# Mycenae-Epidaurus

## Argos-Tiryns-Nauplion

Publishers: George A. Christopoulos, John C. Bastias
Translation: Kay Cicellis
Managing Editor: Efi Karpodini
Art Director: Angela Simou
Special Photography: Spyros Tsavdaroglou, Nikos Kontos and Makis Skiadaresis
Colour separation: Pietro Carlotti

# Mycenae-Epidaurus
## Argos-Tiryns-Nauplion

A complete guide to the museums and archaeological sites of the Argolid

## S.E. IAKOVIDIS, Ph. D.
### Professor of Archaeology

**EKDOTIKE ATHENON S.A.**
**Athens 1994**

ISBN 960-213-035-0
Copyright © 1978
by
EKDOTIKE ATHENON S.A.
1, Vissarionos Street
Athens 106 72, Greece

PRINTED AND BOUND IN GREECE
by
EKDOTIKE HELLADOS S.A.
An affiliated company
8, Philadelphias Street, Athens

# CONTENTS

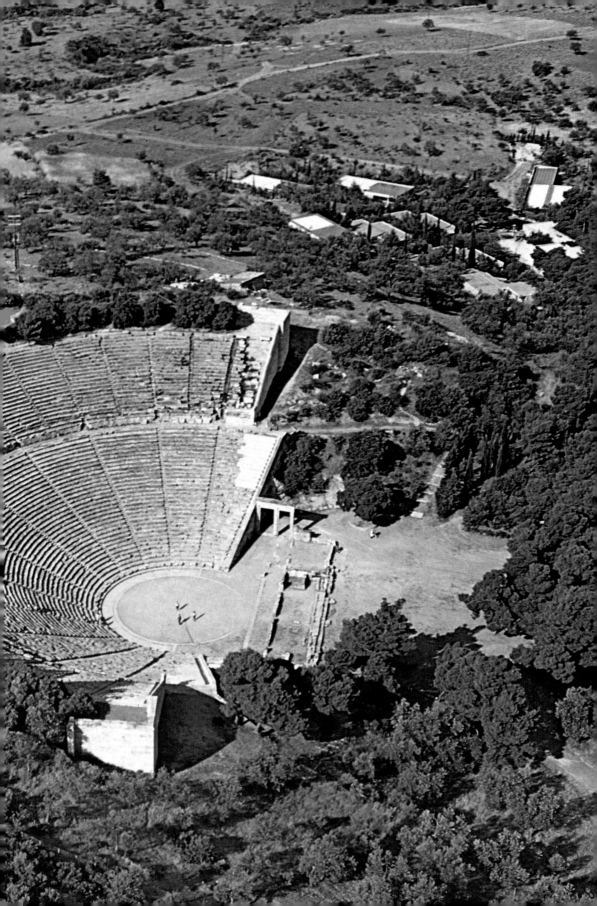

1. The theatre of Epidaurus. General view.

1a. Vase-painting of the 6th century B.C. This depicts the fourth of the twelve labours imposed upon Heracles by Eurystheus, King of Tiryns. The hero has captured the Eryman-thian boar alive and is bringing it on his shoulders to Eurystheus, who is so terrified that he takes refuge in a large storage jar. (Paris, Musée du Louvre.)

# INTRODUCTION

## LAND AND HISTORY

Inhabited without interruption since the very beginnings of prehistory, the Argolid has been sometimes the cradle and sometimes a mere vehicle of the successive civilizations that flourished in Greece. It was also the centre of all those great myths of antiquity that found expression in the epic poetry, drama and art of the ancient Greeks and coloured their intellectual life and political thought. Danaos and his fifty daughters, the adventures of Perseus, founder of Mycenae, the tragic dynasty of the Atreids, the labours of Heracles, the Trojan war — all these ancient tales which made up the sacred history of the Greeks in classical times and survive to this day at the root of innumerable aspects of western culture, had as their natural setting and starting-point the "horse- breeding" and arid plain of Argos and the barren mountains that surround it.

The Argolid consists of a small triangular plain by the sea, about 14 km. wide along the shore and 21 km. deep. Politically and culturally it also includes a rather irregular peninsula, Hermionis, which is situated south-east of the Argive plain and consists of Mount Didymon and some lesser mountains. Hermionis is divided into small valleys; surrounded by the barren islands of Hydra, Dokos and Spetsae, it serves on the eastern side as a breakwater to the deep, narrow sheltered bay of Argolid and its relatively shallow waters and sandy inlets, which provided ideal anchorage for the ships of antiquity.

The plain of Argos is surrounded by a series of mountain-ranges that separate it from Corinthia and the plateaus of Arcadia, and cut off the Hermionis peninsula from the Isthmus region and the deepest recess of the Saronic gulf. On the western side, its borders are defined by the steep slopes of Mount Ktenias (Krios), Mount Malevo (Artemission), Mount Lyrkeion and Mount Pharmaca. On the northern side, there are Mounts Megavouni and Tretos, and on the north-eastern side Mount Arachnaion.

The passes connecting Argolid to the surrounding regions of the Peloponnese are few and rugged: a coastal road along the site now called Kyveri, leading to Thyreatis and Kynouria; two western passages leading to Tegea and Mantineia; the Mount Tretos pass (Dervenakia) leading to Corinthia; and the road that follows the southern slope of Mount Arachnaion, leading to Epidaurus and the Saronic gulf. The mountains gradually dissolve into lesser eminences, ending up in rocky hills on the fringes of the plain, such as Prophet Elias and Zara (Mycenae), or protruding suddenly like solitary islands in the midst of the plain, such as Larisa and Aspida, near Argos, or as the hills of Midea and Tiryns.

The plain is stony along the fringes and reaches to the coast, which is even today marshy is several places. The soil is thin and deficient in iron. From the start this determined two basic features of the Argive plain which remained

2. *Vase-painting of the 5th century B.C. Ajax and Odysseus are quarrelling over the arms of Achilles, which can be seen in the lower middle part of the picture. Ajax, who is brandishing a sword in his right hand, is being restrained by two Greek chieftains. Odysseus on the right is just drawing his sword, but Agamemnon steps between the two men to separate them. (Vienna, Kunsthistorisches Museum.)*

3. *This South Italian red-figure pelike of the mid-4th century, shows the meeting of Electra and Orestes at Agamemnon's tomb. Electra is seated in a position expressing deep despair at the base of the funeral monument. On the left Orestes stands with a phiale in his right hand, preparing to pour a libation on the tomb. (Paris, Musée du Louvre.)*

4. *A vase-painting of the late Archaic period depicting the murder of Aegisthus by Orestes. Orestes, finding Aegisthus seated on the throne of the assassinated King Agamemnon, grasps him by the hair and kills him with two deep sword-thrusts into his heart. Both have their faces turned towards Clytaemnestra, who is approaching menacingly. (Vienna, Kunsthistorisches Museum.)*

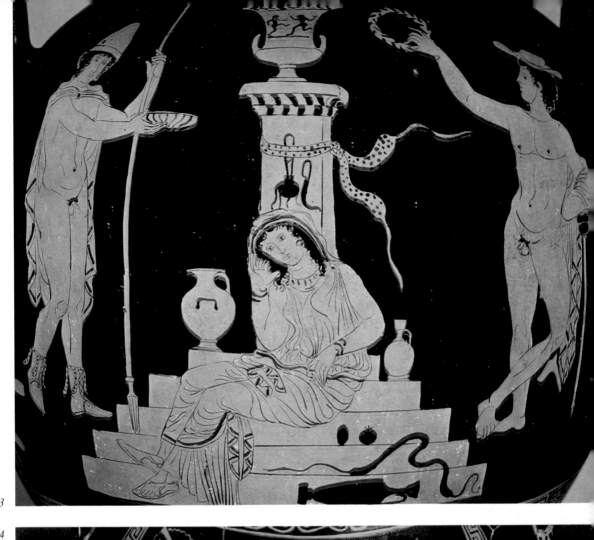

3

4

unchanged until recently, when extensive irrigation works were carried out in the area: a seasonal, surface cultivation, and high quality pottery made of pure yellowish or light red clay. Both these characteristics contributed decisively towards shaping the output, commerce and art of Argolid, particularly in ancient times when it had a closed, localized economy.

The Argolid has no surface water, except in winter. Rainwater is channelled through numerous gullies and forms torrents that reach down to the plain, where they are absorbed by the fine soil; they usually end up as subterranean streams before they have time to evaporate or merge into the sea. This is why there are so many small torrent beds, most of which converge on the bay of Nauplia, without quite reaching the coast; only one of these cuts across to the coast of Asine, while two larger streams, the Charadros (or Xerias) and the Inachos (or Panitsa), descend from the Arcadian mountains, the latter being the only torrent that does not disappear into the plain, but reaches the sea and retains water till the beginning of summer. Subterranean waters abound. They occasionally emerge on the surface of the plain, but also in the sea, as at Anabalos, for instance; but generally speaking, they gather underground at various depths, where they become accessible either by means of wells — of which there was a profusion in ancient times — or deep drilling, this method having become practicable only in recent years.

Argolid thus forms a small, self-contained geographical unit, relatively self-sufficient in the context of a limited, undeveloped economy, closed in, though not totally isolated from the surrounding country, and open to the sea, more specifically to the south and east Aegean and the Cyclades.

The general aspect and the regional centre of Argolid changed in accordance with the particular structure and orientation of each cultural phase in Greek history. During the Mycenaean age, Argolid was the key-point of communications between the eastern Mediterranean and the Greek peninsula and North Europe, its main centres being Tiryns on the coast and Mycenae on the passage towards the Isthmus and mainland Greece. In ancient times, when the whole of Greece was split up into small, independant or semi-dependant city-states, Argolid was an autonomous state centering around Argos, which maintained — within the intricate fluctuations of the balance of power at the time — the permanent role of Sparta's opponent. Later, the Franks and Venetians, having settled in an alien environment and depending therefore on overseas contact with their homelands, found it necessary to build fortresses in Argolid and to fortify the harbour of Nauplia. The Turks allowed the region to fall back into a relatively slack structure based on farming and cattle-breeding, with Argos as a commercial centre and Nauplia as the seat of administrative power. Nauplia was also chosen as the temporary capital of the newly-formed Greek state after the War of Independence.

The oldest human vestiges in the Argolid have been found in the cave of Franchthi, on the west coast of the Hermionis peninsula. They belong to the Stone Age, which covered the period from 20,000 to approximately 4500 B.C. The last phase of this period, the Neolithic Age, ending approximately in 3000 B.C., is represented by a number of other sites in the Argive plain: Mycenae, Berbati, Prosymna, Tiryns, Lerna. Population was denser during the Early Bronze Age (known as the Early Helladic era: 2800-1900 B.C.), about which our principal sources of information are Lerna, Tiryns, Asine, Argos and Mycenae; the main characteristic of this period is the appearance of small, well organized, sometimes fortified, settlements, frequent contact with the sea, and strong Cycladic

5. *Excavations carried out in 1967-1969 at the Franchthi cave, in Ermionis, brought to light an entire phase of Greece's prehistoric culture, including many artifacts dating from the Mesolithic era (ca. 8th millennium) buried in layers of soil four metres thick.*

influences. The flourishing, vigorous civilization that developed in the Argolid during this period underwent a radical change in character and orientation at the beginning of the 2nd millennium, with the arrival of the first Greek-speaking tribes that invaded Greece, initiating the era that became known as the Middle Bronze or Middle-Helladic Age. The new arrivals spread across the whole region and settled in most of the places already used by their predecessors; they brought with them a peculiar type of pottery, monochrome (Minyan) or with a very simple and sparse decoration (matt), and a frugal, almost skimpy way of life, based on farming and cattle-breeding, without any familiarity or contact with the sea. However, the vicinity of the sea, the long maritime tradition of the older inhabitants and the explosive expansion of the Minoan civilization of Crete soon offered the new settlers attractive prospects which they were quick to take advantage of. There is unquestionable evidence concerning the development of communications between Argolid and Crete, Egypt and the Eastern Mediterranean, as well as mainland Greece and the northern areas of the Balkan peninsula; contact was tentative at first, but rapidly grew more intensive and continuous.

The change in the whole cultural climate soon became apparent; one of the main signs of this change was the progressive reinforcement of precisely those centres which were situated at crucial points of the trade routes: Tiryns on the coast, and Mycenae on the passage to Corinthia, the northern Peloponnese and mainland Greece. The final preponderance of Mycenae in this respect was only to be expected. Though Tiryns was the terminal-point of sea-transport, Mycenae was in the advantageous position of also controlling road transport and the hinterland. The land of Argolid provided the raw material for admirable pottery, created under the stimulus of Minoan influence, but reaching their final characteristic form thanks to the ingenuity and imagination of local potters; other craftsmen were also quick to adopt and adapt Minoan and other foreign methods whenever the need arose. Under Mycenaean rule, as far back as the 15th and especially the 14th centuries B.C., the Argive plain became the springhead and focal point of every manifestation of Helladic civilization, which for this very reason has been named Mycenaean. This was where the fortified palaces, known as citadels, were first built and gradually took shape, this was where most of the choicest products of the Aegean and the Middle East were gathered; and it was from the Argolid that most exports (mainly pottery) were exported to neighbouring countries. Furthermore, though written sources are lacking, there exist clear signs of a continuous flow of ideas and mutual influence with the surrounding world.

In no other part of Greece was this civilizing impact so evident and so intensive. From 1600 B.C., when the Mycenaean culture first appeared, in all its power and originality, until approximately 1100 B.C., the Argolid was the centre

*6. Drachma from Argos, 370 B.C. Head of Hera, showing the goddess wearing a polos decorated with anthemia. Trihemidrachma from Epidaurus. Reverse: Asclepios with the sacred serpent. 4th century B.C. (Athens, Numismatic Museum.)*

of Hellenic civilization to the same extent as Athens in historical times, but without concentrating under its immediate political domination the totality, or even the largest part, of the geographical expanse that was Greece, as was the case with Pericles' city. As the epic poem reminds us, the king of Mycenae was the most powerful among the Achaean sovereigns, but not their overlord.

Several other secondary centres developed in Argolid along with Mycenae and Tiryns; they were connected by a dense and well-made road network, interspersed with bridges and control-stations, which led beyond the realm to Corinthia and the Saronic coast.

From the early 12th century B.C. onwards, the citadels lost their great power, and the region was gradually abandoned as successive waves of emigrants left for the eastern Aegean and according to tradition, for Crete as well; this was a severe blow to Argolid, more so perhaps than to any of the other regions of Mycenaean Greece. Between 1100 and 1075 B.C., the once powerful and prosperous state reverted to a phase of limited local rural production that was barely sufficient for the subsistence of those few inhabitants who had remained behind, together with the new settlers, the Dorians. The ingenious, daring Mycenaean warriors, craftsmen and tradesmen were now succeeded by the new arrivals, dull, slow farmers without any political ambitions or interests beyond the boundaries of their farm and the succession of the seasons. The sea was forsaken, contact with the outer world lost its former importance, and the centre of gravity was transferred to the middle of the plain, which was the most propitious point for collecting and exchanging products and for manufacturing and selling those few, simple wares and tools necessary to its cultivation. This was how the ancient settlement at the foot of Larisa first came into being; in two or three centuries, it was to develop into the capital of the region. From the 9th and 8th century B.C. onward, the history of Argolid becomes permanently and indissolubly bound to the fortunes of its sovereign city, Argos.

However, the change in population did not bring about any truly radical alterations to the principal manifestations of civilization. One can perceive, of course, a general restriction of means and techniques, as well as a tendency toward simplification; but the type of housing as well as burial customs remained basically the same. Ceramists, in particular, continued to use the shapes and decorative themes of Mycenean times, or rather simpler variations which became crystallized into abstract Geometrical designs, thus causing both the style and the period to be named "Geometric". This development occured in several Greek regions at the same time, whether the inhabitants were Dorians or not; but Argolid was certainly one of the principal originators of this style.

During the Geometric period the small and relatively impoverished city of Argos was ruled by kings who were descendants of Hercules's great - great-grandson, Temenos. Their sovereignty did not extend far beyond the city boundaries. It is well-known that the ancient Mycenaean centres (Asine, Tiryns, Mycenae, Nauplia), in spite of their decline and financial difficulties, were independant and autonomous cities. However, the gradual increase in the population of Argos, as well as a relative improvement of its financial status, which was mainly due to occasional contact with the far more prosperous cities of the Near East, gave Argos enough strength and confidence to attempt and succeed in subjecting the settlements of the plain, as a result of which it became one of the powers to be reckoned with during that period. Asine was the last to be occupied by Argos; even Sparta's speedy assistance could not save it. This clash was the first in an endless series of conflicts between the two Peloponnesian powers which only ended with the Roman conquest. Total supremacy over the surrounding region and undying enmity towards Sparta were the two basic guidelines of Argive policy over the ages; these were the determining factors in the formation of alliances (with enemies of Sparta, invariably) and expansionist ventures (against Sparta or her federate states). From the start, the apple of discord was the region of Thyreatis, later to become known as the plain of Astros, as this was the main point of access from Argolid to Laconia.

Astros originally belonged to Argos; this was in the mid-7th century B.C., a period of great prosperity and power for Argos. This was mainly due to the efforts of Pheidon, who brought to the city an unquestionable, though ephemeral, glory; later historians have tended to magnify this considerably, just as they have overstated Pheidon's contribution to the economic organization of Argos. He was certainly not the first ruler to introduce weights and measures or to mint coins, as tradition would have us believe. The fact remains that his policy led to a clash with Corinth later on, and this in turn caused Argos to be restricted within its plain until the end of the 6th century B.C.

There followed a period of steadiness, robustness and relative calm, which gave the Argives a chance to organize their city according to the models of the age. Kingship was abolished; throughout the 6th century B.C. a series of tyrants (men who seized power without possessing hereditary rights to it) succeeded each other, until finally authority came into the hands of the *demos*, the people, in other words the privileged free citizens who ruled the entire population of the city and Argolid.

In spite of its political power, Argos did not have much to contribute in the field of culture. Argive ceramics were an imitation of what was being done in Attica and Corinthia; in architecture, Argos could display nothing to compare with the edifices of Athens, Aegina and Corinth; its only remarkable contribution was in the art of sculpture: the statues of Cleobis and Biton at Delphi were the work of the Argive sculptor Polymedes, and there were sculptures by the famous coppersmith Ageladas, of which nothing has survived.

The 5th century B.C. brought a series of fluctuations in the destinies of Argos. In 494 B.C., Cleomenes, king of Sparta, succeeded in taking the Argives by surprise and annihilating their entire army, though he did not occupy the city itself. At a later time, Argos desisted from participating in the Persian wars, not only out of weakness, but also as a result of its opposition to Sparta.

The great earthquake of 464 B.C. that devastated Sparta and led the Messinians to rise in revolt for the third consecutive time, allowed the Argives to reorganize themselves, destroy Mycenae and Tiryns, regain mastery of Argolid and become once more a power to be reckoned with. It was only natural that Argos should have aligned itself with the Athenians during the Peloponnesian war, at the cost of repeated incursions from the Spartans.

The peace of Antalcidas, which dissolved all existing alliances and excluded any future coalitions between Greek cities, left Argos without allies. Weakened by the bloody conflict between the oligarchs and the democrats in 370 B.C., it would have been in serious danger if the Thebans had not definitively checked the power of Sparta at Leuctra. This new phase of Theban sovereignty allowed the Argives to recover and secure their hold on Phlius and Epidaurus, which they had been in danger of losing; they went over to the camp of Philip the Macedonian (and then Alexander), thus ensuring their dominance over the whole plain and their recovery — at long last — of Thyreatis.

The quarrels of Alexander's Epigones repeatedly turned Argolid into a scene

7. *Very little has survived of the architecture of the Geometric period. This perfectly preserved terracotta model of a temple, found at the Argive Heraion, gives a reliable picture of what the earliest Greek temples looked like. (Athens, National Archaeological Museum).*

of strife, the most serious instance of which was Pyrrhus' attempt to master it — an attempt which ended with his death. As regards the rivalry between the Macedonians, the Spartans and the Achaean League, Argos maintained the passive stance of a powerless onlooker. The last confrontation of Argos with its hated enemy took place when the Spartan king, Nabis, invaded Argolid in 197 B.C., occupied and systematically looted Argos and established a garrison within the city walls. Once again, the minor settlements of the plain, such as Mycenae, found an opportunity to rise in arms. However, the joint intervention of the Achaean League and the Romans succeeded in ousting the Spartans once and for all; Argos returned to the League as an independant member until 146 B.C., at which time it was conquered by the Romans, as was the rest of Greece.

Until the 4th century B.C., Argolid led a peaceful life, devoid of political initiative or adventures, with the exception of the violent incursions of the Heruli (A.D. 267) and subsequently Alaric's Goths (A.D. 395-396), who devastated the country and very nearly wiped out the city of Argos itself.

Argolid, on the whole, did not contribute much to the shaping of Greek civilization in the 5th century B.C. under the leadership of Athens, or to the final flowering and explosive expansion of this civilization during the Hellenistic period. The work of the poetess Telesilla (early 5th century B.C.) and the historian and traveller Socrates (Hellenistic period) only present a limited, local interest. There were no Argive ceramists worthy of mention, and this at a time when the whole of Greece was copying the Athenians as faithfully as possible. In sculpture alone, the tradition of Ageladas was continued by his son and apprentice Argeiadas, by Glaucus and Dionysios (known for their statues of gods and poets dedicated to the temple of Zeus at Olympia), and principally by Polycleitos, who was active in the latter half of the 5th century B.C. and created the gold and ivory statue of Hera at Olympia, the *Doryphoros* (spearman), who became known as the *"Canon"*, because it portrayed the perfect proportions of the male body, and the *Diadumenos*. He also wrote a treatise on sculpture. The last noteworthy Argive artist was a relative and perhaps a descendant of Polycleitos. He was named Polycleitos the Younger, and he was both architect and sculptor (one of his works was the statue of Zeus Meilichios at Argos); he worked for a spell at Epidaurus, among other places.

During the first millennium B.C., the population of Argolid was perhaps larger than during the Mycenaean era, but the inhabitants were concentrated in a smaller number of centres, all of which were situated on the fringes of the Argive plain. The old settlements of Mycenae, Tiryns, Nauplia and Asine had developed into small townships *(comae)* which went through alternating periods of vassalage and independance, but always remained self-sufficient. After 468 B.C., yet another small town was added to these; it was known as Alieis, and was near the modern resort of Porto-Cheli. This was where refugees from Tiryns settled when their city was destroyed by the Argives. Apart from these small towns, which all had their own places of worship, there were also some large independant sanctuaries, centres of pilgrimage which attracted people from the whole of Greece, such as the Heraion, the sanctuary of Hera, the principal deity in the region, the sanctuary of Asclepios at Epidaurus, founded near the earlier sanctuary of Apollo Maleatas, and the sanctuary of Asclepios at Troizen. The road network that connected all these religious centres was sparse and elementary as compared to Mycenaean roads. It was dotted with control-towers or simple control-posts, some of which have survived to this day (Kefalari, near Argos, Castro, Asine, Kazarma.)

During Byzantine times, the Argolid was incorporated into the Peloponnesian theme, and the exploitation of the region was systematically organized. The state promoted and reinforced the institution of free farmers and small landowners in the villages of the plain, newly-founded for the most part, and introduced two new products, cotton and silk, to the cultivation pattern of the region. The see of the bishops of Argolid alternated between Argos and Nauplia. Eventually Nauplia became the cathedral city of the Argolid. At the beginning of the 13th century, the Peloponnese fell into the hands of the Frankish Crusaders, who had overthrown the Byzantine state and occupied the whole of Greece. Though Leo Sgouros, ruler of Argolid, put up a stout resistance, the region was finally conquered by the bands of Geoffroy de Villehardouin and William de

Champlitte, and became one of the fiefs of the Peloponnese under the sovereignty of Otho de la Roche, lord of Athens; but with the passage of time its liege lords changed repeatedly. The Franks built a number of castles and citadels especially at Argos and Nauplia where they finally settled; this was due just as much to their sense of insecurity among an alien and hostile population, as to their adherence to ideas and practices current in their distant home countries. The rapacity of Frankish rule soon caused the region to fall into decline and to become depopulated. The void was filled up by Albanians who arrived in Greece in successive waves during the 14th and 15th centuries, and who were rapidly assimilated by the Greeks, in spite of their different language. In 1460, the Peloponnese, including the Argolid, was conquered by the Turks, with the exception of Nauplia, which the Venetians succeeded in retaining until 1540 and in recapturing later (1686-1715). Their mastery of Nauplia, however, was restricted to the city, the harbour (which was their main concern) and the fortresses. The Argive plain, divided into great estates (recognizable to this day under their old place-names, such as Passas, Avdibey, Djeffer-aga), belonged for the most part to the Turks, whereas the Christians — at least, those who were not serfs — made their living from farming and from the few miserable flocks of sheep and goats they could afford to feed. The Turkish pasha resided in Nauplia, but the urban centre, the focus of production and trade and cottage industries — particularly as far as the Greeks were concerned — was Argos, which was protected by a number of special privileges (for instance, the Argives were not forced to give hospitality to visiting Turks); it was not long before it became the main Greek city in the Peloponnese.

Towards the end of Turkish rule, the Argolid began to attract various foreign travellers who visited the sites of antiquity and tried to identify their ruins, and who were also in the habit of carrying away quite a number of "souvenirs" in the course of their peregrinations. During the War of Independence (1821), the Argolid was frequently the scene of war operations, such as the destruction of Dramalis pasha's army at Dervenakia, the siege of Nauplia, and the checking of Ibrahim's progress at Myloi. In 1822, Nauplia became the seat of the revolutionary government, and following the liberation of Greece, it was made the capital of the new state under governor John Capodistrias and later under king Otto, until 1834, when the capital was moved to Athens.

The Argolid now forms a separate administrative department of prefecture (nomos). Its main livelihood is farming, but it has also developed into one of the principal tourist centres of Greece. It is connected by land with the rest of the country by the national road which begins at Corinth, passes through Dervenakia, leaving Mycenae on the left, and crosses the plain in order to end up at Argos. To the east of this road, we come across the Heraion and Midea, which can be reached by local roads via Mycenae or Argos. At Argos the main road branches in two directions: the continuation of the national road leads to Myloi (Lerna), situated west, and then climbs up the hairpin bends of the Achladocampos towards the plateau of Tripolis; to the east, the road bypasses Tiryns and reaches Nauplia, where another branch runs along the length of Mount Arachnaion, ending at Epidaurus via Ligourio, and continues via Karatza along the coast to Troizen, Methana and Galata (on the opposite shore from Poros); finally, yet another branch, heading south-east, goes through Asine (Tolo) and Iria and then turns south, through Kranidi, and ends up at Porto-Cheli and Costa, on the shore opposite Spetsae. Kranidi is connected with Galata by a road that also passes through the little coastal town of Hermione.

# MYCENAE

The palace of Mycenae was built on a relatively low hill, 278 m. above sea-level and 40-50 m. above the surrounding plain. The houses and tombs were situated all around the palace. There are two other higher, abrupt hills on either side, Prophet Elias to the north (805 m.) and Zara (660 m.) to the south. Two deep and precipitous ravines, the Kokoretsa on the Prophet Elias side, and the Havos on the Zara side, isolate the hill of Mycenae, allowing access only from the western slope.

Tradition has it that the founder of Mycenae was Perseus, son of Zeus and Danae; it was he who had the mythical Cyclopes — the builders of Tiryns — erect the walls of the citadel for him, which for that reason became known as Cyclopean walls. Perseus' grandson, and the last king of this line, was Eurystheus, who set Heracles the task of performing his famous twelve labours, and who was killed in Attica without leaving any descendants. The Mycenaeans chose as his successor his brother-in-law, Atreus, son of Pelops, who proved a good ruler and did much to strengthen Mycenae. However, his enmity towards his brother Thyestes led him to give the unfortunate man the flesh of his own children to eat (the so-called Thyestean feast). This deed brought upon Atreus and all his descendants the wrath of the gods and Thyestes' curse: his son and heir Agamemnon, who assumed the leadership of the Greeks on the expedition to Troy, was slaughtered on his return from the war by his own wife, assisted by her lover, Aegisthus; Orestes, the son of Agamemnon, and his sister Electra killed both their mother and Aegisthus, after which Orestes was forced to flee, pursued by the Erinnyes, until he finally was acquitted by the Areopagus. The last king of Mycenae, according to tradition, was Tisamenos, Orestes' son; he was killed while defending his country from an incursion by the Heraclids.

It is no easy task to discern the kernel of historical truth that lies buried under these tales. It seems fairly certain, however, that the roots of Mycenae were far more ancient than the ancient Greeks could remember; their memories did not reach further than the 13th, or the 14th centuries B.C., at the very most. We know that the hill of Mycenae and the surrounding hills had been inhabited without interruption from as far back as the Neolithic age; but the first important vestiges — several walls and, above all, the extensive cemetery on the western slope of the hill including the royal burial enclosures at its two extremities — belong to the middle of the 2nd millennium B.C. There was surely a palace as well, which was subsequently buried under later constructions and which at first we can assume was not walled. The first fortifications, which converted the palace into an acropolis, were built circa 1350 B.C., but they acquired their present aspect not earlier than 1200 B.C. During this period, Mycenae was the seat of the powerful kings of the region, who apparently ruled the greater part of Argolid and perhaps even the whole north-east region of the Peloponnese. They

*8. The acropolis of Mycenae with its Cyclopean walls. It was built on a naturally fortified eminence overlooking the Argive plain.*

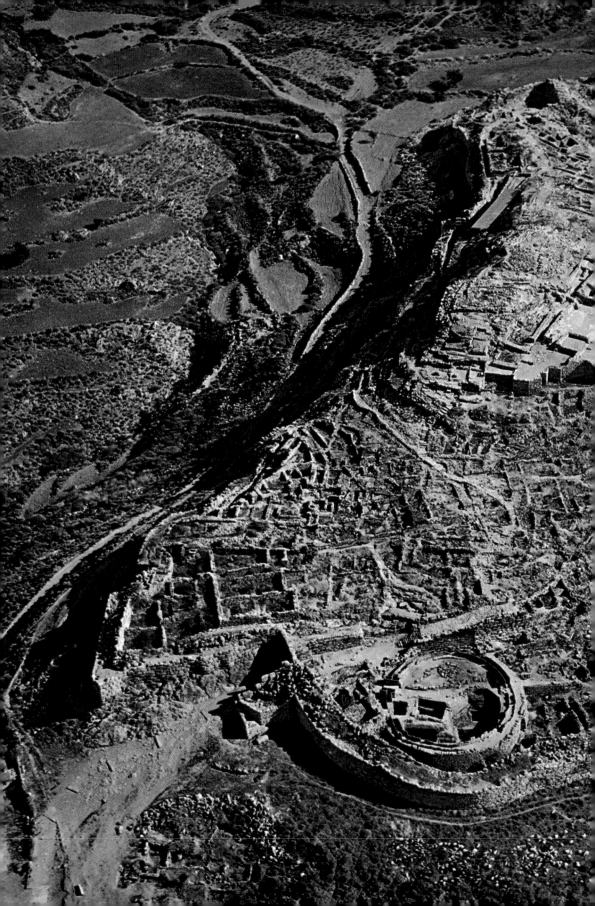

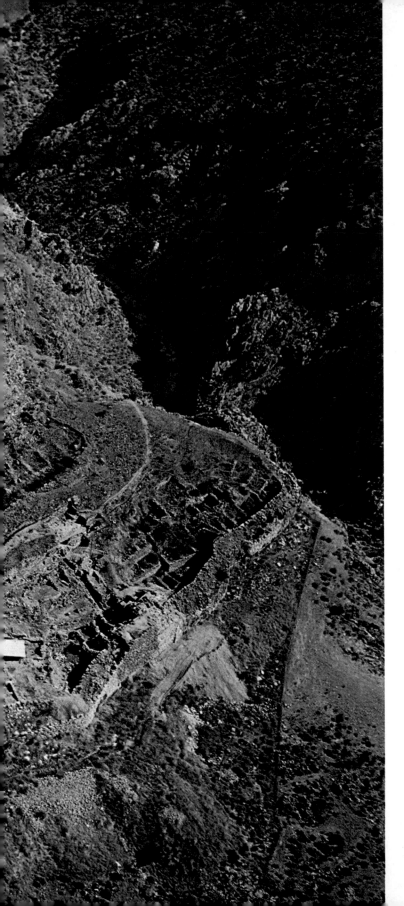

9. *Aerial view of the acropolis of Mycenae showing the walls, the Lion Gate, the grave circle A and the ruins of the palace at the top of the hill.*

23

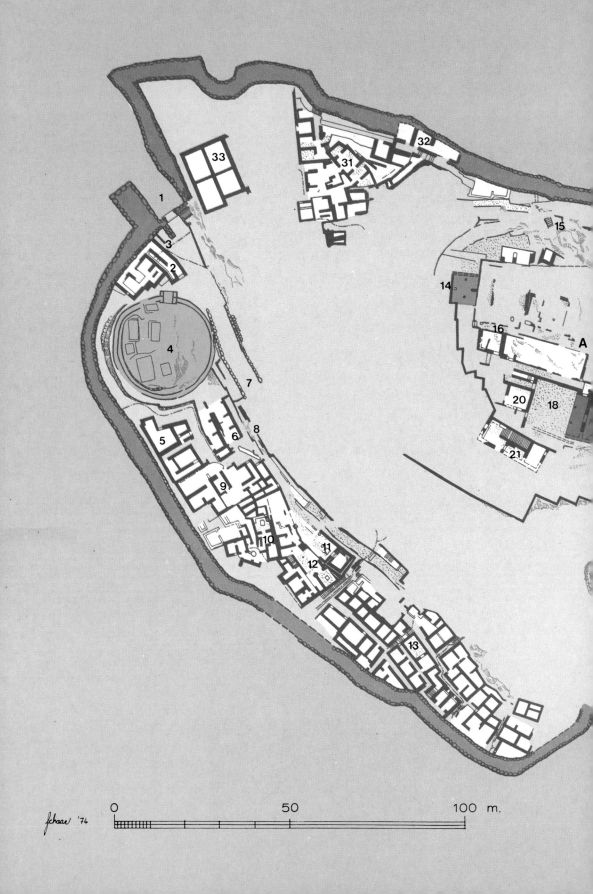

schaar '74

0     50     100 m.

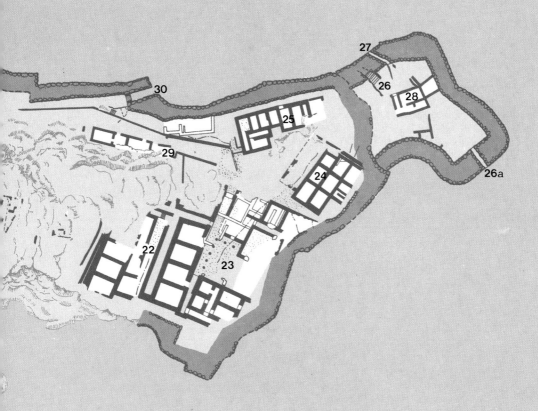

# Plan of the acropolis at Mycenae

1. Lion Gate
2. Granary
3. Straircase
4. Grave Circle A
5. House of the Warrior Krater
6. Ramp house
7. Great Ramp
8. Small Ramp
9. South house
10. Sanctuaries
11. Adyton
12. Tsountas' house
13. Buildings

A. Palace
14. Propylon of the palace
15. North ascent
16. North corridor of the palace

17. Bathroom
18. Great court
19. Megaron
20. Square room
21. Grand straircase
22. Workshop of the artists
23. House of Columns
24. House D
25. House Γ
26. Undergound fountain
26a. Sally port
27. Exit
28. Houses A and B
29. Rooms (store rooms)
30. North gate
31. House M
32. Store rooms
33. House N.

directed the economic life of their realm and kept up contacts with abroad. Excavations have shown that until about 1200 B.C. the ascendancy of Mycenae increased and its power expanded steadily. The historical fact which lies behind the epic poems on the Trojan war (most probably a Greek attempt to settle permanently on the north-west coast of Asia Minor) should be ascribed to that period. A number of fires that broke out in the palace and various buildings within and without the acropolis were followed by repairs, reconstruction and a normal continuation of life. But then came gradual decline. The standard of living fell apace, foreign contacts diminished, and in 1100 B.C. the acropolis of Mycenae was burnt down and abandoned, and the various buildings within its walls eventually collapsed. However, the region was still inhabited by a mixture of descendants of the old Mycenaeans and the newly arrived Dorians. Later in the Geometric period, several small houses were built on the ruins of the palace, but were then covered up by the large Archaic temple (of Athena?) that was erected on the top of the hill, thus destroying the Mycenaean vestiges to a considerable extent. The fortification walls survived. In 468 B.C. the Argives took the acropolis and destroyed its fortifications at various points, only to repair them in the 3rd century B.C. when they founded a new town which occupied the whole fortified area as well as that beyond the walls. This town survived till the Roman period, but not as late as Pausanias' time (2nd century A.D.). Pausanias' description is the last we hear of Mycenae before antiquarians and treasure-hunters of the 18th and early 19th centuries discovered the site (Lord Sligo, Lord Elgin), and carried away at various times a number of objects, especially from the treasury of Atreus. Excavations began properly speaking only after the emergence of the modern Greek state. In 1841, the Archaeological Society uncovered the Lion Cate, which had been buried up to the lintel; in 1874 Schliemann conducted a few tentative soundings; in 1876 he discovered the circle containing the royal shaft graves within the acropolis (Grave Circle A) and excavated five of them, as well as the tholos tomb known as the tomb of Clytaemnestra. In 1877, P. Stamatakis, curator of antiquities, excavated the sixth, and last, shaft grave in the circle. From 1880 to 1902, Ch. Tsountas, on behalf of the Archaeological Society, investigated the whole area thoroughly and brought to light the palace, several buildings and the underground fountain within the acropolis, as well as numerous tombs outside the walls. His work was carried on by Wace (1919-1923, 1939 and 1950-1956), who was in turn followed by Lord William Taylour until 1966. Meanwhile, the Archaeological Society resumed its activities. At first these were limited to restoration work. But in 1952, after the discovery of the royal grave circle outside the walls (Grave Circle B), the Society took over the task of excavating the tombs and various points on the acropolis and the surrounding area. Since then, research has continued uninterruptedly by Professor G. Mylonas.

The result of all this research work is Mycenae as we see it today: between the two tall, steep hills, lies the citadel containing the palace, various other buildings and Grave Circle A. Outside the walls, at the foot of the citadel and over the surrounding hillocks, there is the continuation of the Middle Helladic cemetery, with Grave Circle B at its western extremity, as well as several buildings, various chamber tombs and 9 tholos tombs. A number of Hellenistic ruins survive among the Mycenaean remains. On the banks of the Havos, to the right of the modern road that leads to the acropolis, part of a Mycenaean road-bridge survives and at several other points, not easily accessible to the visitor, there are remnants of similar bridges and traces of Mycenaean roads.

## THE ACROPOLIS

**The fortifications.** With the exception of three sections which were destroyed by the Argives and restored at a later date, the fortification wall is Mycenaean in its entirety. It was made of two kinds of stone: the façades of the Lion Gate, the North (or Postern) Gate and a shallow bastion on the south-east wall (in front of the House of the Columns) were all built of large ashlar conglomerate blocks placed in alternate courses. Conglomerate (Schliemann's breccia) was used at the main points of the fortifications which needed to be emphasized, but, generally speaking, the walls were made of untrimmed boulders, larger on the façades and smaller for the core of the walls; they were put together without any binding agent forming perfect joints, sometimes evened out by small stones in the interstices (Cyclopean system). Hellenistic repairs (such as the curved section on the Lion Gate bastion and the adjacent piece of the west wall, the "polygonal

*10. Part of the fortification wall at Mycenae. In the background is the Lion Gate, the entrance to the acropolis, with its massive lintel surmounted by a relieving triangle.*

*11. The acropolis of Mycenae: a reconstruction of the fortification wall
and the palace at the top.*

tower'' in front of the House of Tsountas and part of the so-called north-east extension) are easily distinguishable because the stone has been cut into polygonal shapes with straight edges fitting each other with perfect precision, without the need of intermediary wedges.

The fortifications of the citadel belong to three different periods: the earlier circuit walls (dating from circa 1350 B.C.) only enclosed the top of the hill, leaving out Grave Circle A; its main entrance must have been just above the Lion Gate. From this first period, only the north part of the wall has survived, pierced later by the northern gate. The rest was demolished, leaving only few and practically undistinguishable traces; and the Lion Gate was then built at a lower level, together with the west and north section that included Grave Circle A (1250 B.C.). A little later (1200 B.C.), an L shaped extension was added to the narrow north-east part of the fortification, the so-called North-east extension, which included the underground fountain of the acropolis. With these additions and extensions, the fortified area came to cover 30,000 square meters, with a circuit wall approximately 900 m. long, surviving to this day almost in its entirety (with the exception of the part above the bank of the Havos). This heavy and impressive enceinte of an average width of 5.50 – 6 m., following faithfully the contours of the rock so that it appears like an organic part of it, has not survived at any point to its full height. We have therefore no indication as to how the top of the wall was formed, though quite probably it was uniform throughout, without any bricks at the top and without ramparts.

**The Lion Gate.** One of the most imposing structures of all times, was the main entrance to the citadel. The approach followed a natural uphill path, leading to a narrow space between the smooth, steep rock on the left and a long, narrow bastion (14.80 m. × 7.23 m.) on the right. At the end of this narrow space, in which the aggressors were forced to huddle together, exposed on all sides to the volleys of the guard, there is the gate, which consists of four single conglomerate blocks. The opening is 3.10 m. high, and 2.95 m. wide at the bottom, narrowing to 2.78 m. at the top. The lintel (4.50 × 2.10 × 1 m. in the middle part, which is the thickest) and the threshold (4.60 × 2.40 × 0.85 m.) each weighs over 20 tons. The two jambs (3.10 × 1.95 × 0.50 m.) are smaller. These enormous blocks, like the stones that were used in the construction of the wall, were rolled to the site on ramps, and the finishing was done on the spot. The threshold shows several cuttings: there are three, slightly irregular grooves, which were thought to have been chariot-wheel ruts, but which were cut at a much later date, in historical times, in order to assist the drainage of rainwater from the inner part of the gate. It is also covered with shallow cuttings to prevent animals from slipping; there is a shallow square hole in the middle of the front edge and a smaller, circular hole further in. These cuttings were all made later; they belong to the Archaic, or perhaps even the Hellenistic period. The only Mycenaean features are two cuttings at the inner angles of the jambs, originally round in shape, but later disfigured; two corresponding cylindrical holes are on the lintel. These accomodated the hinges of the door-panels: two rounded, vertical beams with protruding ends which rotated within the holes as the panels of the door opened or shut. The jambs have a kind of projecting border on their outer surface, about 0.10 m. thick, continued along the length of the lintel; this formed a frame that stopped the panels of the door from swivelling outwards. On the inner side of the jambs, there are two square holes; they accommodated the ends of a square, wooden bolt which kept the door securely shut. Other oblong

12. *The Lion Gate at Mycenae. The imposing stone relief from which it takes its name —
two lions, three metres tall, facing each other over the massive lintel — lend an air of
rugged grandeur to the acropolis entrance. It is the earliest example of Greek monumental
sculpture.*

holes, two on each jamb, were probably meant to receive the handles of the
door-panels so that the door could be pushed wide open.

In order to relieve the lintel of some of the weight of the superstructure, the
ashlar courses at both its ends which are supported by the door jambs, corbel out
progressively leaving a triangular empty space — the so-called relieving triangle
— which is a kind of simple arch characteristic of Mycenaean architecture. For
practical as well as aesthetic reasons, this empty triangle was filled in with a slab
of hard limestone bearing in relief two lions after which the gate was named.
These are the earliest example of monumental sculpture known to us in Europe.
The lions stand erect, facing each other, with their front paws on two small
concave altars. Their heads, which were apparently shown frontally, have not
survived; some traces left on the slab panel indicate that they were made of
some heavy material, possibly steatite. On the two small altars and between the
lions, there is a column that supports part of the entablature of a building. This
shows that the column was not meant to represent a deity (as Evans and Wace

*13. A view of the acropolis of Mycenae showing the successive fortification walls built of Cyclopean masonry, which consists of huge irregular blocks of stone.*

believed) but symbolizes a building, most probably the palace itself, the royal house of Mycenae, which the lions had been appointed to guard. The relief is therefore more or less the equivalent to a coat of arms of later times. Although executed in low and somewhat stylized relief, its plastic planes and surfaces are very marked and carefully executed; in spite of the symmetry of the representation, its robust and sufficiently naturalistic style cannot but impress the visitor and clearly symbolizes the power and prestige of the palace of Mycenae.

Beyond the gate, there is a small square courtyard, which was originally roofed; it is flanked on the right by a free-standing wall and on the left by the rock, masked by a conglomerate facing. This facing has a small niche, which was thought to have been used by the guard of the gate or to have housed a watch-dog, but has now been unquestionably identified as the gate sanctuary, similar to those discovered on other ancient sites. On the right of the courtyard,

*14. Aerial view of the acropolis of Mycenae, showing Grave Circle A, the Granary, the Ramp and the pathway leading up to the palace.*

there is a structure named the Granary, which is built against the inner side of the fortification wall, and Grave Circle A. The Great Ramp, in front of them leads up to the top of the hill and the palace.

**The Granary.** This structure is narrow and cramped, and its façade was evidently planned in relation to Grave Circle A, which shows that it was built later than the circle. It is built of masonry on a stone terrace fill; only the ground floor has survived, and there were found a number of jars containing carbonized wheat, which gave the building its name, although it is more probable that it was used by the guard of the gate; there are vestiges of the upper floor, which communicated with the store-room by means of an inner staircase, of which only the first two stone steps remain. None of the brickwork of the upper floor walls has remained in place. On the north-east side of the building — facing the courtyard of the Lion Gate — there are two narrow parallel corridors that led to the upper floor of the Granary and were extended, at a later stage, on a slightly different axis; the joint is clearly visible. The Granary was built at a late date and was in use up to the final destruction of the citadel. Its pottery, and generally speaking, the class to which it belongs is known as the Granary Class and is typical of the last years of Mycenaean civilization.

**The staircase.** Between the Granary and the righthand wall of the Lion Gate there is a small, square, stone-paved space which housed a staircase leading to the top of the wall; it was discovered under a pile of rubble which was all that remained of the staircase and the neighbouring structure, and which contained pottery similar to that found in the Granary. Only the floor-paving survives today. The various architectural fragments lying on the floor do not really belong here, but come from buildings of the Hellenistic period.

**Grave Circle A.** Originally — i.e. in the 16th century B.C. — this consisted of a group of large shaft graves, unquestionably used for royal burials. They were dug on the slope of the eastern end of the Middle Helladic cemetery of Mycenae, and were enclosed by a low circular rubble wall of which only a very small section has remained. The building of the Lion Gate and the west fortifica-tion wall, at a much higher level, relegated the tombs to the bottom of a large, artificial hollow, practically inaccesible, and possibly dangerous, owing to the waters that gathered there. In order to bring the burial ground to the level of the acropolis entrance, a stout, battered wall was built on the slope over the old enclosure, to retain the fill which covered the graves. This wall levelled the ground artificially, and was topped by upright slabs of soft stone — sandstone and shellstone — forming two concentric circles, at a distance of approximately 1 m. from each other. The slabs were of equal height, and the interval between the two circles was roofed by similar, horizontal slabs supported by small wooden posts (some of which have been restored and can be seen next to the entrance of the enclosure). Thus the slabs form a circular, apparently compact parapet. On the north side, near the Lion Gate, there is an entrance with three threshold slabs, between two square cross walls which terminate the circle on both side.

The enclosure contained six large royal shaft graves, numbered from I to VI, and a number of ordinary graves, small and shallow, which were destroyed in the course of the Schliemann excavation, except for one, discovered by Papadimi-triou in 1956, half-covered by the slabs of the parapet. Schliemann excavated five out of the six graves; Stamatakis excavated the sixth grave, nearest to the entrance; the inner row of the parapet slabs passes across the angle of this grave. All six were family tombs; they are large rectangular pits measuring from 3 × 3.50 m. (II) to 4.50 × 6.40 m. (IV). On other side, the tombs had low rubble walls upon which lay horizontal beams that supported the roof of the grave, about 0.75 m. from the floor. The roof was made of slate slabs or wattle (reeds and weeds), covered with an insulating layer of clay. The dead were buried at the bottom of the pit, and the dug-out soil was piled on over the roof; finally the place was marked by an upright stone stele, either plain or adorned with relief work. The burial was followed by a funeral banquet; the remains of the meal were covered up with a few handfuls of soil. Whenever a new burial was about to take place, the stele, the covering soil and the roof were removed and then put back into place. Various objects belonging to the dead, known as *kterismata*,

*15. Poros funeral stele from Grave Circle A at Mycenae, with relief decoration consisting of a row of spirals in the upper part and a hunting scene or chariot race below. (Athens, National Archaeological Museum.)*

were buried along with the corpse; these grave gifts were particularly abundant and sumptuous in the graves of Circle A. They are now exhibited at the National Archaeological Museum of Athens. They indicate that the dead were buried fully clothed and adorned; some had their faces covered with gold masks, thus betraying a certain superficial Egyptian influence, as did a number of other objects. Apart from the masks, mention should also be made of the gold vessels and jewels, of the bronze swords with gold and ivory hilts and of the daggers decorated with gold and silver inlaid blades that were found in the tombs. It has been estimated that the 19 dead in Circle A (eight men, nine women and two children) were buried with not less than 15 kgs. of gold; at least eleven stelae were erected on the tombs, of which some survived whole and others in fragments. They had already been removed from their original position when the later circle, contemporary to the Lion Gate, was built in the 13th century B.C.; it is therefore not possible to ascertain whether the sculptured stelae were destined to the men and the plain ones to the women, as some scholars have maintained. According to the evidence supplied by these and other Mycenaean tombs, burial customs seem to show that in spite of the opulence of grave goods and the obvious reverence for the tombs themselves, Mycenaeans did not practise a cult of the dead.

16. *Reconstruction of Grave Circle A at Mycenae, showing the outer fortification wall and the ruins of adjacent buildings.*

17. *The stairway and great ramp leading up to the palace on the acropolis of Mycenae.*

Directly south of the Circle one finds the remnants of two buildings: the first, on a lower level than the second, has an indented surface, hugging the curve of the terrace wall of the enclosure, which means that it had been built at a later date. Only two rooms, separated by a passage, remain today; they have strong rubble walls covered with mud plaster reinforced with straw and mud. Schliemann, who excavated this structure, believed it to be part of Agamemnon's palace. It has no connection, however, with the palace of Mycenae; but was the basement of a small building which was destroyed at the same time as the Granary, and which contained the fragments of a large Late Mycenaean krater decorated with figures of warriors (National Archaeological Museum of Athens); the building was therefore named "the **House of the Warrior Krater**". Higher up, on the extension of the terrace supporting Circle A, there are some poorly preserved remains of walls belonging to another structure, known as the **Ramp House** because it was erected at the foot of the Small Ramp (see below). One can barely discern a kind of megaron-shaped room flanked by three smaller rooms, possibly store-rooms. The fresco known as "Women at the Window", now at the National Archaeological Museum of Athens, was discovered here.

**The Great Ramp.** As the visitor makes his way back to the inner courtyard of the Lion Gate, he finds himself in a narrow open space, with the Granary and the Grave Circle on his right, and a transversal wall on his left; this wall supports a narrow terrace stretching along the length of the steep rock face, interrupted by a few steps (recently put there to replace the ancient ones) that lead to the wall overlooking the Lion Gate. Directly ahead of the visitor, following the axis of the Lion Gate, the visitor will see the Great Ramp, the starting point for the ascent to the palace. It is a Cyclopean structure, with a low parapet on the right and a 20% inclination which indicates it was made only for pedestrians. The ashlar wall concealing the face of the rock on the left belongs to the Hellenistic period, but it was built over an older, Mycenaean wall, made of mud bricks with timber framing. Originally the Great Ramp was narrower and less steep, thus allowing a passage towards the houses next to the Circle parapet. However, at some time before 1200 B.C., it was broadened till the foundations encroached on one or two slabs of the parapet, and the passage was consequently obstructed. In order to establish communication with the area south of the Grave Circle, a second, smaller ramp was built as an extension of the Grand Ramp; this led to the top of the Great Ramp, at the same level as the buildings. The passage connecting between the two ramps was built over and deformed, during the Hellenistic period, by a series of rooms; their foundations are visible to this day.

From the top of the Great Ramp, the visitor has a general view of a whole series of structures built on the slope of the hill, along the length of the wall, right up to the banks of the Havos. The first structure, immediately after the House of the Warrior Krater, has been named the **South House,** as it was situated at the southernmost point of the excavation area at that time; beyond this house there are several rooms which have been named **Citadel House,** but which are really no more than an extension of the South House. Many of the brick walls have survived as a result of the fire, which destroyed the building, baking them at the same time into hard bricks which kept the traces of the timber framing that originally reinforced them.

Beyond the South House, between the fortification wall and a processional road skirting the length of the slope, there is the group of *sanctuaries* belonging to the Mycenaean citadel. The road begins with a number of stone steps, followed by a well-cut threshold (half-concealed now by a Hellenistic wall), that is by a door which shows that it was originally roofed, and then forms a bend, and leads to a square space which has the foundations of a square altar at its entrance and a large flat stone (a slaughtering stone) inside; next to it, there is a horseshoe-shaped plaster hearth, which is now kept covered as a protective measure. Behind the hearth, there is a small square room, which was probably the *adyton,* the inner sanctuary of the temple. At a lower level, there is another building known as the **Tsountas House** (after the name of its excavator), which consists of a courtyard, a ground floor apartment divided into a vestibule and an inner hall, and a series of basement rooms connected with the courtyard by a stone staircase. In front of the Tsountas House there is the **Temple of the Idols,** thus named from the clay idols of snakes and deities of the nether world that were found in it, now exhibited at the Museum of Nauplia. This temple is also now kept under protective cover; at a lower level, extending to the wall, there is another complex of rooms which contained frescoes representing various deities (Museum of Nauplia). In front of these rooms there is a forecourt with a round hearth plastered with yellow clay. The group of sanctuary buildings is separated from the houses further south by a stone staircase next to an open drain descending towards the wall, which was repaired at this point during the Hellenistic period. The polygonal façade and the flat terrace with a small cistern at the top also belong to the Hellenistic period. From there on, the buildings succeed one another along the slope; they are separated vertically by steps and drains, some open and some covered by the steps, and horizontally by narrow, more or less straight lanes. In one of these rooms near to the Tsountas House and next to the wall, the magnificent frescoes of the *"Mycenaean Lady"* and the great eight-shaped shields were discovered; they are now in the Mycenaean Room of the National Archaeological Museum of Athens.

The uphill path that leads from the top of the Great Ramp to the palace, passing between the walls and foundations of structures belonging for the most part to the Hellenistic period, is of very recent date. The old Mycenaean ascent has disappeared without any recognizable traces. However, the conformation of the rock is such that it could not have differed much; but the end of the path, which now leads across the propylon of the palace, was certainly elsewhere. The path probably branched into two separate sections that ended up at the two entrances to the palace, north and south.

**The palace.** Built at different levels on the top of the hill, the palace complex of Mycenae is founded on an extensive area of artificially levelled ground, supported by massive Cyclopean terraces. The northern retaining wall was rebuilt, in historical times, but the western and southern sections retain their original aspect. There were other similar terraces supporting the east wing of the palace, overlooking the Havos.

The palace was originally divided into three parts. The topmost section was destroyed and totally buried under the foundations of the Archaic and Hellenistic temples that were successively built on that spot. The foundations of the Hellenistic temple are still to be seen together with a few scattered architectural fragments. Very few and barely distinguishable vestiges of the Mycenaean structures (probably the domestic quarters) have survived. The middle section of the palace, a long and narrow expanse between two passages, called the north and south corridors, has also been intensively dug into and damaged. Apparently it was a terrace facing south, overhanging the third and lowest part; this included the state apartments. In spite of the great fire that destroyed it, enough has survived to indicate clearly the arrangement of the rooms and the details of construction; this enables the visitor to form a clear impression of the spaciousness and grandeur of Mycenaean palatial architecture.

The entrance to the palace was situated on the north-west corner, at the point where the present path ends. It has a *propylon* that preceded the entrance proper. The floor was at a much higher level than it is today. There was a central door and two columns standing along its axis; their bases have been restored to their original position. To the north, the propylon overlooked a small, stepped terrace, which was the landing where the *northern ascent* to the palace led; before reaching the propylon the ascent went past a double guard room built at the foot of the north terrace wall. From this north ascent to the palace, which was closely adapted to the contours of the rock, only a few steps remain in a crevice; lower down, the stairway to which they belong has been destroyed by a Helleni-

*18. The ruins of the palace at the top of the acropolis of Mycenae (aerial view).*

stic wall. A few sections of the retaining walls that supported the pathway leading to the propylon have also survived, together with some vestiges at the bottom of the wall indicating that the beginning of the uphill path was originally looking in the direction of the main entrance to the acropolis. Thus when the North Gate was built at a later date, the lower landing of the ascent was made to face in that direction as well.

In ancient times, as the visitor climbed the ascent and crossed the propylon, he emerged into a narrow passage along the west retaining wall; from there he could follow, turning left, the *northern corridor* of the palace which would lead him directly to the upper quarters, or he could proceed a little further and reach the point where a large conglomerate threshold survives; there are also vestiges of two lateral walls framing the threshold; this has become known as the *Western Portal*. From that point, the ancient visitor could follow the south corridor and end up in a narrow room with benches built into the wall and a staircase that led to the upper quarters. This part of the palace also includes a room of which only a corner has survived, with traces of red plaster on the floor; it has been fancifully identified as the *bathroom* in which Agamemnon was murdered. If one turns right directly after the portal and proceeds along a short and narrow passage, one ends up in the *great palace courtyard* (15 × 12m.); its floor was decorated with multi-coloured stucco (it is now covered up). On the north side, the courtyard is enclosed by a wall made of regular ashlar blocks, initially bound together with a timber frame (later destroyed by fire) and faced with plaster, of which no traces

41

remain. To the south, there was a low parapet allowing a general view of the Argive plain; to the west, there was a number of rooms and to the east the main *megaron* of the palace, of which the south-west section has tumbled down into the Havos together with the corresponding section of the terrace and the fortification wall that overlooked the ravine. This part of the wall has been restored.

The *megaron* consists of a columned porch, a vestibule (*prodomos*) and the main chamber (*domos*). The shallow porch (3.85 × 11.50 m.), opens to the courtyard: it has two columns on the front side, a floor made of gypsum slabs, and a small passage on the left leading to the room with the benches and the staircase; a large single-panel door led to the vestibule; only the threshold has survived, made of a single block of conglomerate with two small square holes at both ends, which were meant to accommodate the wooden posts of the jambs. The vestibule (4.30 × 11.50 m.) had a floor of painted stucco bordered with gypsum slabs, and a doorway leading to the megaron, similar to the one described above, but without traces of a door; it was probably hung with a curtain instead. The *domos,* almost square in shape (12.96 × 11.50 m.) was the principal room in the palace, where the king's throne was placed. The floor was also decorated with coloured stucco and bordered with gypsum slabs on all four sides, and the walls were covered with frescoes (National Archaeological Museum of Athens). In the middle of the room, there was a large, round hearth (3.70 m. diameter, now covered up as a protective measure); its painted stucco surface was renewed ten times, but the decorative motifs of flames and spirals remained unchanged. The hearth was encircled by four wooden columns, coated with bronze, which supported the roof; their stone bases have survived; the north-west base, fallen in Havos ravine, has been replaced in its original position. In accordance with the arrangements in the megara of other Mycenaean palaces, the throne must have stood in the middle of the south part of the room; but nothing remains of it. Opposite the megaron, on the west side of the court, there is a *square room* with two adjacent doors leading to a forecourt that communicated with the court and the Grand Staircase. The substructure of the forecourt has covered, at this point, an earlier basement, which has become known as the *Pillar Basement.* The *Grand Staircase* (not open to the public) was the second official access to the palace, and was added at a later date. It was a four-sided structure which contained a spacious, imposing staircase divided into two flights, a stone one, which has survived, and a wooden one, which was destroyed. The wooden flight of stairs rose along and above the stone flight and reached a landing that crossed over the top of the staircase to lead into the forecourt of the square room. In other words, the visitor to the palace who climbed this staircase reached the court of the megaron, by way of its neighbouring forecourt. This seems to confirm the theory (Tsountas, Mylonas) that the square room and the space lying to the west of it (its walls have barely survived) were guest rooms intended to house official visitors of the king, and not the throne room (as Wace assumed), which was undoubtedly situated in the domos of the megaron.

To the east of the remains of the Mycenaean palace and of the foundations of the Hellenistic temple, built with various earlier materials, the surface of the hill is now quite bare. However, a careful study of the site has shown that here too, it had been arranged into successive terraces descending towards the banks of the Havos and the outer fortification wall; the east wing of the palace, separated from the rest by a curved corridor, was founded on these terraces. The only surviving remains of the east wing are the buildings on the lower side of the hill; but they have been partially destroyed and altered by the houses of the Hellenistic township built over them in the 3rd century B.C. The first building that meets the eye on the right as one comes down the hill is a square edifice (28 × 30 m.) consisting of two rows of rooms, built on two different levels; they are separated by a long and narrow courtyard on both sides of which run two corridors. A few surviving steps show that there was a staircase here leading to a second floor over the lower east wing. The entrance to this building, on the north-west corner, was completely destroyed by the Hellenistic foundations, easily discernible as they are at an angle to the Mycenaean walls. The finds of the 1965 excavation indicate that this building was the **workshop of the artists** and **craftsmen** working for the king. Between the workshop and the east Cyclopean wall, there is another building with a central court surrounded by a colonnade (hence the name **House of Columns**) which communicated with the workshop and similarly belonged to the palace. The only remains are the basements and the foundations of the ground floor, which are unfortunately deformed by a Hellenistic wall that cuts across them. However, one can still see quite clearly the entrance marked by the bases of the door jambs, made of conglomerate (one of these still shows traces of the saw with which it was cut) and the wide threshold of the outer door. Crossing this threshold one enters a narrow passage which ends in the central court, on the north side of which there is a large square megaron-like room, which was later divided into smaller rooms. Opposite, the basement store-rooms still survive; this is where one of the few inscribed Linear B tablets of the citadel were found. The House of the Columns was the principal building of this palatial wing, but it has not been possible to determine with any certainty what kind of purpose it served.

The entrance of the building faces a small triangular square, now stripped down to the surface of the rock. There are two other structures on either side. One of these, built against the inner side of the east Cyclopean wall (**House Delta**) had a terrace in front of its façade, with a drain covered with paving-stones running across it. The other building (**House Gamma**) was erected along the north wall, from which it is separated by a narrow passage. Only the basements of these two structures have survived, and here again there is no way of knowing what purpose they served. Like the palace, these buildings were destroyed by fire in 1200 B.C., but they were repaired and continued to be used until the citadel was finally abandoned.

Having passed between Houses Gamma and Delta and reached the lower part of the rocky eminence, the present pathway leads to the north-east extension, which was the last to be added to the fortifications of the hill; this took place in the late 12th century B.C., not so much with a view to increasing the fortified area as to ensure a continuous supply of water for the citadel. Fresh-water springs existed — and exist to this day — on the hills east of the citadel; there was no difficulty in channelling the water through conduits up to the foot of the hill, but there was no way of cutting the hard rock in order to provide a cistern within the fortified area. The only suitable place for the construction of an underground **fountain,** at a deep enough level to keep it safe from attack (about 18 m.) was a crevice in the rock at the north-east corner of the old wall. However, the opening leading down to the fountain had to be placed inside the fortified area, and this is the reason for which the north-east extension was built. Like the rest of the wall, it was adapted to the contours of the rock and encircled a small piece of flat, level ground which had remained unfortified until then. The descent to the fountain cuts across the wall of this later addition; under the shelter of a corbel vault, it leads down to a Cyclopean portal, the lintel of which, cracked at the left end, is supported by a monolithic pillar. The portal opened on a landing, followed by the rest of the descent, which is divided into two sections. The second section has its walls coated with hydraulic mortar and ends up in the underground fountain, which was supplied with water from the spring by means of a pipe system. (After the portal, the passage down is very dark, so visitors should be equipped with torches.)

The wall of the north-east extension — Cyclopean with Hellenistic repairs — was added to the older wall in such a way that the joints are visible. At the south end of the wall, the lower courses of the old wall continue well within the extension. At two points on the north and south sides, vaulted openings cut across the wall. The one on the south side, which is the largest, was thought to be a secret emergency exit *(sally port);* but it is quite visible even from a great distance, and led to an outer terrace overhanging the banks of the Havos. The opening on the north side is transversal, low and narrow; once believed to have been a drain it was really an *exit* leading to the springs and to the North Gate. These two openings greatly facilitated communications with the area east of the acropolis and were easily blocked up in case of a siege.

Within the north-east extension were discovered the foundations of two Mycenaean buildings (**Houses A** and **B**) and next to the north part of the wall, a circular Hellenistic cistern.

On the way back from the north-east extention, having crossed the triangular square, the visitor can now proceed along the pebble-strewn path that goes past a row of *rooms* leaning against the steep rock-face, which serves as their back wall. These rooms, now fenced in with barbed wire, had two storeys; they were totally destroyed by fire. In the basements, which alone have survived, were discovered several jars (those damaged beyond repair have been replaced by exact replicas, collected from other parts of the citadel). The store-room is directly above the North Gate; it is reached by a flight of steps, badly damaged and recently restored.

**The North Gate.** The North Gate was a faithful replica of the Lion Gate; it was built in an opening deliberately made into the north wall for this purpose. On the one side, a bastion made of conglomerate blocks (6.54 m. long and 3.25 m. wide) was built parallel to the opposite section of the old wall. A narrow passage was thus formed in between them (2.30 m. wide), similar to the outer courtyard of the Lion Gate, and the gate was erected at the end of it; here again the frame consisted of four conglomerate blocks. On either side of the threshold and lintel one can still see the pivot holes intended for the hinges of the double panelled wooden door (the Restoration Service has installed exact replicas in their place), as well as the two holes in the jambs for the great wooden bolt that kept the door shut. The only difference between the North Gate and the Lion Gate is that instead of the relieving triangle above the lintel, there are two conglomerate slabs with an empty space between them (which helps to relieve the weight considerably) and with a slightly convex lower surface, so that only the two ends rest upon the lintel, where it is supported by the jambs.

On the inner left side of the gate, there is a small sanctuary inside a niche, as at the Lion Gate. The staircase leading to the store-room and the north-east extension goes over this niche. As we go past it, we have on our right the north wall and on our left a series of retaining walls; we then cross a relatively narrow passage (interrupted here and there by Hellenistic walls) and reach the landing at the foot of the north ascent to the palace at the end of the pathway that connected

*19. The north postern of the acropolis at Mycenae. An opening was specially made in the north wall to enable this gate to be built.*

it with the Lion Gate. Further on, along this pathway, and to its right among a dense tangle of walls and rooms that are for the most part ruins of the Hellenistic town, another Mycenaean building **(House M)** stands near the north wall; the ground floor was divided into four rooms, and it had a well made staircase (six sandstone steps) leading to the upper floor. The entrance to the ground floor is at the north-west corner of the building, and it is flanked by a double porter's lodge. The building was erected on artificially levelled ground, and was separated from the north wall by a deep, narrow passage. At the east end of this passage there were several *store-rooms,* of which three (barely discernible today) were built right inside the wall. Next to the store-rooms, along the extension of a road that went past House M, there is another similar, but smaller, room, with a corbel roof and a double drain running under its floor; some scholars have compared this room to the vaulted galleries at Tiryns.

Above the Lion Gate, a rectangular building was cleared, consisting of four square rooms, which were the basements of yet another Mycenaean building **(House N).** The remaining buildings in this area have not yet been systematically investigated. From House N one can return to the Great Ramp or go down directly to the inner court of the Lion Gate by the curved flight of stairs that has been recently restored, thus concluding the visit to the acropolis.

## THE AREA SURROUNDING THE CITADEL

The ancient monuments around the acropolis are mostly tombs, belonging to various types and periods, and intended for various classes of people. There are also a number of houses, but they are still too few to show the arrangement and extent of the Prehistoric, or even of the Hellenistic, settlement of Mycenae. The older tombs, dating from the 17th and 16th century B.C., are shaft graves, as in Grave Circle A; the later ones, dating from 1500 B.C. onwards, are tholos (or beehive) tombs for royalty and chamber tombs for the common people. In the 2nd century A.D., Pausanias voiced an opinion that was common in his time: he named the tholos tombs *"treasuries"* — meaning the treasure-houses of Atreus and his descendants. Contemporary local tradition, on the other hand, ascribed to the tombs the better-known names of members of the Atreid dynasty. Thus the tombs have totally arbitrary appellations such as "the treasury (or tomb) of Atreus" (or "Agamemnon", "the tomb of Clytaemnestra", "the tomb of Aegisthus", "the tomb of Orestes", and so forth. Other tombs have been named after their location or some typical find connected with them.

As the visitor walks down from the Lion Gate towards the modern entrance to the site, he can leave the enclosed area, turning right, and come upon one of the tholos tombs, known as the **tomb of the Lions** (owing to its vicinity to the Lion Gate). On either side of the *dromos* (the long passage leading to the tomb), which is 22 m. long and 5.40 m. wide, one can still see the regularly cut, ashlar blocks of poros stone that faced the wall. The entrance (5.40 × 2.40 m.), decorated with a shallow, double fascia and topped by a quadruple lintel, leads into the chamber (14 m. diameter). The inner walls consist of regular courses of field stones, except for the sides of the entrance and part of the foundations, where ashlar conglomerate was used. The floor was dug out of the natural rock. There are three plain pit graves, which were found empty, as was the rest of the tomb. The tholos has only partly survived, up to the height of the lintel; it is estimated that it must have been about 15 m. high. The tomb was built ca. 1350 B.C.

To the left of the Lion Gate, the road goes past the foundations of a long, narrow, rectangular Hellenistic structure, known as the **Perseian Fountain House** mentioned by Pausanias. Behind this fountain and between the Lion Gate and the modern motorway lies the Middle Helladic cemetery of Mycenae, of which the two royal circles are to be seen. At a later date, two tholos tombs were built here, now called the **tombs of Aegisthus** and **Clytaemnestra.** The first tomb, farthest to the east, was built circa 1500 B.C., which makes it one of the oldest tholos tombs at Mycenae. It has a long and narrow *dromos* (22 × 4.50 m.), with a wall-facing made of untrimmed stones. Its original facade, framing an entrance 5 × 2 m., was built in a similar way, and so were the inner walls of the chamber. A second, purely decorative façade, built of ashlar conglomerate and poros blocks, was added later, masking the earlier one entirely. It survives now only on the right jamb and at the bottom of the left jamb.

The side walls of the entrance are bent out of shape as a result of the thrust of the superstructure, combined with the weight of the fill and have now been shored up with wooden props. The chamber has a diameter of 13 m. Its original height would have been approximately the same, but the upper part of the tholos has now collapsed. It contained only one pit, near the entrance, and was despoiled as far back as the Hellenistic period. The second tomb, Clytaemnestra's, lying west of Aegisthus' tomb, was built approximately 250 years later, i.e. circa

20. The tunnel leading down to the underground fountain at Mycenae.

21. The tholos tomb known as the "Tomb of Clytaemnestra". The side walls of the dromos are built of ashlar conglomerates. At the end of the dromos is the façade of the tomb, with the door way and the relieving triangle above it.

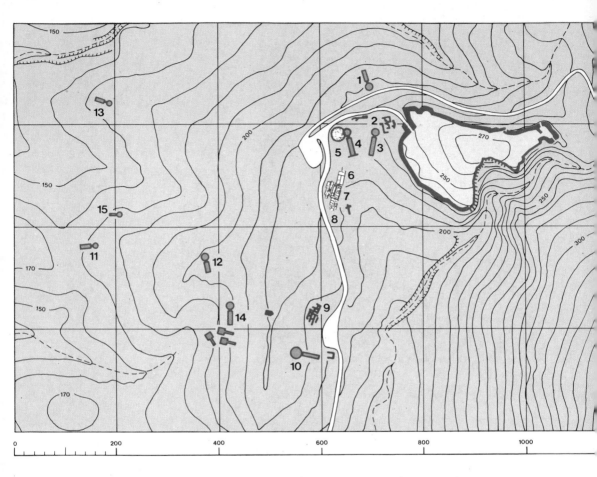

## Plan of the area surrounding the citadel

1. *Tomb of the Lions*
2. *Perseia fountain house*
3. *Tomb of Aegisthus*
4. *Tomb of Clytaemnestra*
5. *Grave Circle B*
6. *House of the Shields*
7. *House of the Oil Merchant*
8. *House of the Sphinxes*
9. *Group of mycenaean buildings*
10. *Treasury of Atreus*
11. *Cyclopean tomb*
12. *Pano Fournos tomb*
13. *Kato Fournos tomb*
14. *Panagitsa tomb*
15. *Tomb of the Daemons of Orestes' tomb*

1220 B.C. During the Hellenistic period, it was buried under the theatre of the Hellenistic township of Mycenae (a row of stone seats from this theatre — the rest were wooden — have survived on top of the dromos leading to the tomb); it was accidentally discovered a short time before the War of Independence and systematically plundered by Veli Pasha of Nauplia. The side walls of the dromos — 37 m. long and 6 m. wide, have a facing of carefully cut and trimmed ashlar conglomerate blocks. The construction of the façade is similar; the doorway is 5.40 m. × 2 m., with a triple lintel lightened by a relieving triangle; only a few traces of the sculptured decoration have survived: left and right of the entrance, one can still see the square bases that supported fluted gypsum half-columns;

over the lintel there were sculptured stone slabs that covered up the relieving triangle; it was blocked from the inner side as well, by means of light rubble masonry. The door had two wooden panels (their pivot holes are still visible) and a threshold of conglomerate slabs, originally coated with wood or bronze. The tholos (13.50 m. diameter) was destroyed at the top when it was plundered, and was subsequently restored to a height of 13 m., in accordance with the inner curve of its walls. The restoration led to the discovery of Grave Circle B in 1951 and this was followed by excavations carried out by the Archaeological Society (I. Papadimitriou and G. Mylonas).

**Grave Circle B.** As it was situated outside the citadel walls, it was not interfered with and retains its original form to the present day. It lies at the west end of the cemetery. It contained 14 royal shaft graves, either earlier or contemporary to the first graves of Circle A, similarly marked by stelae, five of which were found in their original position, while one or two had been moved. This group of tombs was enclosed by a thick, low, circular wall of rubble masonry, 28m. in diameter, like Grave Circle A, which included, apart from the royal tombs, another twelve graves, small and shallow, intended for ordinary citizens or perhaps palace officials. All the graves have been marked with letters of the Greek alphabet. The larger tombs are similar as those in Grave Circle A; but in this case careful excavation has given a much clearer picture of structural details and burial customs, thus elucidating many of the queries which Schliemann's excavation had left unanswered. The largest tomb — *Grave Gamma* — is 3.80 × 2.80 m., and was found to contain the bones of three men (one of whom had a trephined skull) and a woman. The other tombs contained the bones of three, two or even one interment only. The grave goods were less opulent than those discovered in Grave Circle A, but they included a mask (Grave Gamma) and some master-pieces of early Mycenaean art, such as the small amethyst seal engraved with a male portrait head (Grave Gamma again), the gold sword hilt in *Grave Delta*, finely ornamented sword blades in *Graves Iota* and *Lamda*, the gold cup of *Grave Nu*, and the magnificent rock crystal vase of *Grave Omicron* (the richest of all), with a handle in the form of a duck's head. After the last burials, the tombs were left undisturbed, except for *Grave Rho* (now covered with a cement roof), which was excavated, emptied and enlarged during the 15th century B.C. in order to accommodate a vaulted chamber of poros stone slabs, with a roofed dromos, of the type known only in Mycenaean settlements outside mainland Greece, such as those on the Syrian coast (Ras Shamra — Ugarit) and Trachona in Cyprus.

At a small distance south of the Circle, along a Mycenaean road winding up to the acropolis, there is a group of four buildings dating from the 13th century B.C., partially destroyed and covered by geometrical tombs and Hellenistic structures. Three of these buildings have been excavated by Wace. They stood in a row on a piece of artificially levelled ground; only the basements have survived. The northernmost structure, known as *the House of the Shields* (it was found to contain small ivory replicas of eight-shaped shields) is separated from the next structure by a stone straircase that led down to the road. The middle building, named *The House of the Oil-Merchant,* consists of a long passage with store-rooms on either side that contained jugs and jars filled with oil, standing on small hearths that kept the liquid warm. The third structure, at the southern end of the group, stood right against the previous one and had a similar design. It was named *the House of the Sphinxes,* after the ivory plaques engraved with sphinxes that were discovered in it. Behind and above the House of the Oil-Merchant, a

22. *Reconstruction of Grave Circle B at Mycenae. It contained 14 royal shaft graves similarly marked by stelae. The positions of Grave Circle A and of the palace at the top of the hill are marked for reference.*

fourth structure was discovered by N. Verdelis, with its ground floor intact. It consists of a paved courtyard leading to a row of rooms and a megaron-type chamber. At the corner of one of the rooms there was a kind of fire-place, much larger than the hearths common at the time, which cut across the width of the wall right into the next room. This fire-place, combined with the jars in the House of the Oil-Merchant and the inscribed clay tablets referring to male and female personnel, oil and perfumes, seems to indicate that these buildings were not merely living quarters, but perfumery workshops, operating either as a private business or for the palace. The whole group of buildings was destroyed and abandoned towards the end of the 13th century B.C.

The houses were built at the foot of the Panaghitsa hill (named after the white-washed chapel of the Virgin — *Panaghia* — standing at the top). About 200 m. to the south, higher up the slope and next to the small asphalt parking-lot, in front of the Atreus tomb, there is another Mycenaean group of buildings which has been only partially excavated. It consists of houses with one central room and hearth, and several auxiliary rooms surrounding it; these are reached by a system of corridors. The only remains are some terrace walls that held up the crumbling soil of the slope and the lower, stone-built part of the houses' walls. Very few and barely discernible traces of the brickwork and timber framing of their upper part have survived. The place has been fenced off and is

*23. The famous tholos tomb known as the "Treasury of Atreus". At the far end of the dromos is the monumental façade of the tomb, with the doorway surmounted by a massive lintel and a relieving triangle.*

not open to the public; but nearest to the barbed wire fence and therefore clearly visible is House I, which is fairly representative of all the others: first, there is a courtyard, then a rectangular vestibule (the prodomos) leading to the domos, which has a hearth in the middle (now covered). At the back, there was yet another room (opisthodomos), and a corridor that ran the length of the rooms. Other rooms, probably auxiliary, gave on this corridor, but they have not been excavated, as they lie under the wire fence and the parking-lot. This house — and most probably, the others in this group — was destroyed in 1230 B.C. by an earthquake, of which one victim was found in the course of the excavation: the skeleton of a woman who had taken refuge in the doorway between prodomos and domos, and was crushed under the ruins of the upper storey.

The hill of Panaghitsa was densely populated at this point. Earlier excavations have revealed vestiges of various buildings (e.g., the *House of Lead*, named after a deformed lead vessel found among its ruins) which show that the construction of the treasure of Atreus entailed the destruction of many other buildings that had to make way for the enormous sepulchral monument.

**The treasury of Atreus (or tomb of Agamemnon).** This is the most splendid monumental structure of Mycenaean architecture of its peak period. Like the Lion Gate, it was built circa 1250 B.C. (not earlier, as has been surmised) and was in use over a long period of time; it is impossible to say for exactly how long. A large section of the hill slope was hewn out for its construction. Carefully trimmed and fitted conglomerate blocks, placed in horizontal, pseudo-ashlar courses, were used for the dromos and the tholos.

At the beginning of the dromos (36 m. long and 6 m. wide), there was a low transversal wall that held back the fill thrown in after each burial. The sides of the dromos were faced with squared boulders, more or less the same size, except for the bottom course, which was made of larger blocks (one of these was 6 m. × 1.25 m.). The rows of blocks rise up to form the monumental façade, 10.50 m. high, with a doorway in the middle (5.40 m. high, 2.70 m. wide at the bottom and 2.40 m. wide at the top), framed by a double, sculptured fascia. The lintel is topped by a relieving triangle. Hardly any of the ornamentation on the façade has survived. Right and left of the doorway there were two half-columns of greenish marble with zig-zag fluting, decorated with spirals, the surviving fragments of which can be seen today in the British Museum and the National Archeaological Museum of Athens, incorporated into reproductions of the façade. The section above the lintel was faced with multi-coloured marble that covered the relieving triangle and consisted of horizontal rows of spirals and half-rosettes, flanked by two half-columns with slanted fluting. Several attempts have been made to reproduce this section, but the surviving fragments are so few that none of the existing reproductions may be considered reliable in all its details. The doorway closed by means of two panels, coated with wood or bronze leaf, that turned over the slabs of the threshold. The inner part of the lintel was of a piece (9.50 × 1.20 m.) and weighed 120 tons; it was cut in such a way as to fit the inner curve of the tholos. The tholos, 14.60 m. diameter and 13.50 m. high, was built of regular square blocks in 33 horizontal rings that still bear the marks of bronze nails here and there; these were meant to secure some additional metal ornaments, probably rosettes. There is a second smaller doorway on the north side of the chamber; it is similarly topped by a relieving triangle, and leads to a square side-chamber, 6 × 6 × 6 m. The walls are now bare and irregular, but they were faced with sculptured stone slabs, and there was probably a central support holding up the horizontal roof. The British Museum has a few pieces of gypsum slabs decorated in relief which may have belonged to the facing of these walls.

The tomb was despoiled in antiquity, and none of its contents have survived: Pausanias tells us that the ancient Greeks believed the tomb to have been the treasury of Atreus and his descendants: this gives us some idea of the opulence of the grave goods discovered in the tomb at the time of its desecration.

On the west side of the hill of Panaghitsa and on the hill range west of it, five more tholos tombs were discovered (the Clyclopean tomb, the Pano Fournos tomb, the Kato Fournos tomb, the Panaghitsa tomb, and the tomb of the Daemons or Orestes' tomb); they are all smaller and less well-made than the ones described above. As they are hidden away among olive-groves and meadows, they are not easy to locate, and anyone wishing to visit them should ask for a guide. The same is true of the various groups of rock-cut chamber tombs, some of which are visible at the edge of the road leading from the village of Mycenae to the archaeological site, near the village's modern cemetery.

*24. Reconstruction of the façade of the most impressive tholos tomb at Mycenae, the "Treasury of Atreus". The façade was elaborately decorated. On either side of the door there stood a half-column of greenish stone with sculptured ornamentation, and the empty space of the relieving triangle over the lintel was originally concealed behind a stone slab with reliefs of spirals and other decorative motifs.*

4

# FINDS FROM MYCENAE
# IN THE NATIONAL ARCHAEOLOGICAL MUSEUM
# OF ATHENS

The excavations on the acropolis of Mycenae and the surrounding area have brought to light a considerable number of objects, the most important of which are today housed in the Mycenaean Room of the National Archaeological Museum in Athens. Most of them are from tholos tombs (the so-called treasury of Clytaemnestra in case 7, for example) or chamber tombs excavated by Tsountas (cases 1, 2, 26). The most impressive, however, are the finds from the shaft graves in the two royal grave circles at Mycenae — Circle A inside the acropolis (cases 3, 4, 22, 23, 24, 25, 27, 28) and Circle B outside the walls (cases 5 and 6). There are vases in a variety of forms and shapes, made of clay, bronze, silver and gold, weapons, tools, jewellery, sealstones, and ornaments that were sewed to the clothes or the shrouds of the dead princes. The gold death masks displayed in separate cases are exceptionally interesting; each portrays a different physical type. The daggers with inlaid decoration and the rhytons in the shape of a bull's head and a lion's head are also fine pieces. The better preserved of the funerary stelae from Grave Circle A stand amongst these cases. The room also contains pottery, figurines, objects of gold and ivory, and also a small number of inscribed clay tablets. These were discovered in the palace, and at various points of the acropolis (case 21, 30), or in the houses (case 31); they are all brilliant examples of Mycenaean art, representing different periods and genres. Amongst them are the carved ivory group depicting two seated female figures with a child between them on their lap (case 30); the female head made of painted plaster; the warrior krater; and the frescoes, especially that of the "Mycenaean lady" — a striking female figure with delicate lines and lively colours (case 19). Finally, the restored relief half-columns from the treasury of Atreus are displayed on the walls of the room.

These exhibits, with their richness and variety, the delicacy of their workmanship and their vigorous shapes and decoration, reflect the robust, warlike, yet refined spirit that characterised the world of Mycenaean Greece.

*25. Plaster head of a woman, possibly a sphinx. The plastic rendering of the facial features is accentuated by touches of brightly-coloured paint on the white surface. It was found in the enceinte of the acropolis at Mycenae, south of Grave Circle A. 13th century B.C.*

26. *Fresco of a female figure, discovered in 1970 by Professor G. Mylonas in a house just inside the west wall of the acropolis at Mycenae. The powerful design, the wide range of colours and the expressiveness of the figure are unique in Mycenaean art. Late 13th century B.C.*

27. *The celebrated Mycenaean "Warrior Krater". On the front, we see six warriors, each armed with a small shield and a spear and clad in chiton, short breastplate and helmet; they are probably leaving for the war. A female figure standing on one side raises an arm in farewell. Late 13th century B.C.*

28

29

28. *Ivory head of a warrior, wearing a helmet reinforced on the outside with wild boar's tusks. It was found in a chamber tomb at Mycenae. 13th century B.C.*

29. *Ivory statuette of two women and a baby, with obvious religious connotations. This exquisite work of art ranks among the masterpieces of Mycenaean minor sculpture. 13th century B.C.*

*30. Small rock crystal vase in the shape of a duck. The rendering of the bird's neck and head and the exceptional delicacy of the carving of the curved line raise the object to the level of a masterpiece of sculpture in stone. It was found in Grave O of Grave Circle B at Mycenae. 16th century B.C.*

33

*31-32. Gold death masks from Grave IV of Grave Circle A at Mycenae, both portraying beardless men. They are of two different types: in the first the eyes are closed and the eyelids clearly visible: in the second the eyes appear to be open, though in reality they are closed. 16th century B.C.*

*33. Gold death mask known as the "Mask of Agamemnon", the most expressive of those found in Grave Circle A. It is a realistic repoussé representation of the face of a leading Achaean king. The mask was found in Grave V of Grave Circle A at Mycenae. 16th century B.C.*

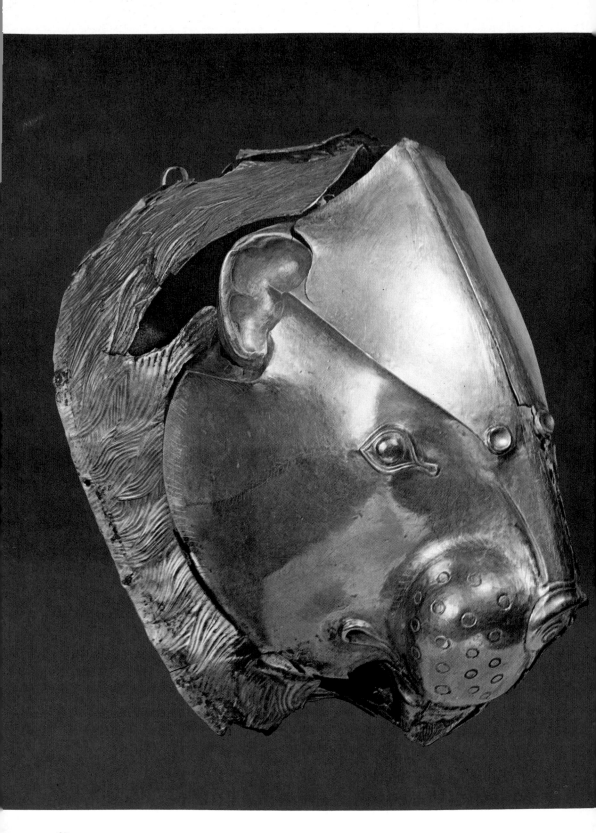

34. Gold rhyton in the shape of a lion's head from Grave IV of Grave Circle A. An exquisite example of Mycenaean embossed work. 16th century B.C.

35. Gold head of a woman, perhaps a goddess, from a silver brooch. There are two floral symbols superimposed on her head. From Grave III of Grave Circle A at Mycenae. 16th century B.C.

36. Gold seal representing a man fighting with a lion. From Grave III of Grave Circle A at Mycenae. 16th century B.C.

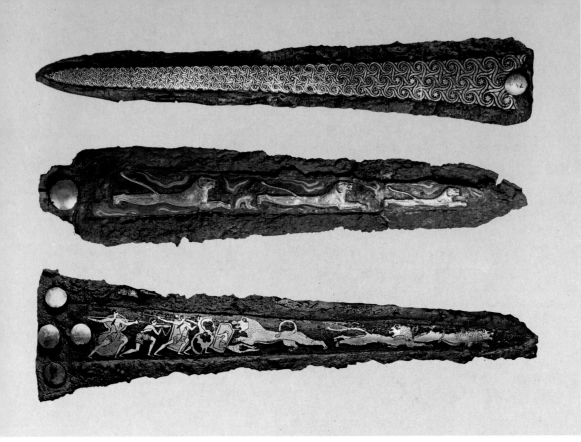

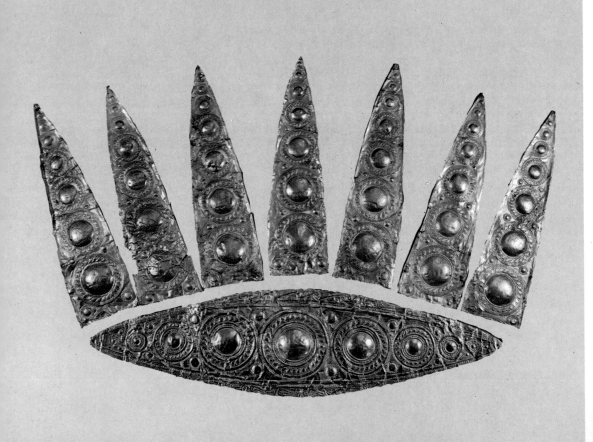

37. *Elaborate bronze daggers with inlaid ornamentation of gold, niello and amber. They were found in Graves IV and V of Grave A at Mycenae. 16th century B.C.*

38. *Gold rhomboid diadem, with flat spear-shaped pieces. It was found in Grave III of Grave Circle A at Mycenae. 16th century B.C.*

39. *Silver rhyton in the shape of a bull's head, with gold horns and a rosette on the forehead. Found in Grave IV of Grave Circle A at Mycenae. A remarkable specimen of the Mycenaean goldsmith's art. 16th century B.C.*

39

# ARGOS

Argos has been continuously inhabited from Prehistoric times to the present day. Consequently, each period destroyed or obliterated the remains of the earlier era, so that what comes to light now are only a few and badly preserved ruins. The town was (and still is) built on the eastern slopes of two rocky hills skirted to the north by the Charadros (Xeria) river bed. One of these hills, the ancient Larissa (now called Castro), is quite steep and has a hight of 289 m. The other hill, much smaller (80 m. high), round-shaped and smooth, crowned by the chapel of Aghios Elias, is generally known by the name of Aspis (it was recently suggested that this was the name given to a section of the Larissa foothills). From the saddle between the two hills, the Deiras pass, started two ancient roads, leading to Lyrkeia and Mantineia.

Argos can boast of no significant modern monuments (except perhaps for the Neoclassical mansion of General Tsokris, at the beginning of Karatza Street). Most of the antiquities that have survived and may be visited were excavated by the French School of Archaeology; they are mainly to be found at three points in the city's area: at the south-western foot-hills of Larissa (where one can see a section of the ancient agora, the theater, the odeum, the Roman baths and the sanctuary of Aphrodite); at the top and at the southern foot-hills of Aspis (wall, sanctuary of Apollo, and perhaps of Athena, Prehistoric settlement, and Mycenaean cemetary); and finally at the top of the Larissa hill (the citadel). There are also some remains of the city's walls, built in the 3rd century B.C. especially near the Larissa and Aspis fortifications.

The **agora** was situated near the modern road to Tripolis (Gounari Street). Of the large complex of ancient buildings (Pausanias mentions 18 temples) erected during the 5th century B.C. and destroyed by Alaric's Visigoths in A.D. 395, only a very small section — the south-western corner built over a Geometric cemetery — has been excavated. At the extreme corner of the complex, the foundations and the walls of a 5th century B.C. building were found revealing a

*40. Larissa hill with the medieval citadel on its summit. In places, some sections of ancient walls are still visible, incorporated in the medieval fortification.*

square-shaped (32.60 m. long) hypostyle structure containing 4 colonnades, each consisting of 4 Ionic columns, of which only the bases have survived. The structure had an eastern entrance giving access to the agora. Next to this building, there was a long and very narrow *stoa* (83.45 × 5.60 m.) which also gave access to the agora and formed its southern flank. Its eastern extremity formed a side wing 23.35 m. long and 10.46 m. wide, with a colonnade on its eastern façade. There was probably a similar western wing, but in any case, the two stoas encompassed a large area, perhaps a palaestra, with which, however, they did not communicate. The stoas were built at almost the same time as the hypostyle structure, which communicated with the long wing by a ramp. After the A.D. 395 destruction, this area was considerably remodelled. The square-shaped building was replaced by baths and the stoa was divided into small shops and stores.

Another Roman building in the agora site, 40-50 m. north of the eastern corner of the stoa, is a circular cistern (*nymphaeum*) with a fountain in the interior and a row of 8 Corinthian columns outside. Finally, about 100 m. north of the agora, at an oblique by-road off Gournari Street, a large house was excavated belonging to the 4th (or perhaps the 5th) century A.D.; its mosaics (now transferred to the courtyard of the Argos Museum) represent Dionysus with his followers and the Months of the year.

The most impressive ruins of the ancient city are to be found south of the agora, on the other side of the road. The closest to the road, and therefore to the agora, are the public baths, or **thermae,** built in the 2nd century A.D. and restored in the 4th century A.D. Its western section, an arched brick structure measuring 23 × 10.60 m., has been well preserved practically to its full height, perhaps because it was later used as a Christian church; however, the pedestal of a statue beneath the arch and a crypt with three tombs carved in the rock under the floor indicate that it had originally served as a heroon. A long and narrow passage (29×7.40 m.) with four entrances leads off from the arch and reaches the main baths (recognizable today by the foundations) giving the structure an elongated shape and an E-W axis. From the entrance, three steps lead down to the long and narrow transversal dressing-room with its built-in benches along the walls and two symmetrical antechambers leading to the large cold water room — the *frigidarium* — with its three pools (one can still see the southern one). From here the bathers went through a small square antechamber and proceeded to one of the three hot chambers (*caldaria*) which had underground heating installations (very well preserved, with their characteristic, closely built, small brick pilasters that supported the floor and allowed the hot air from the furnace to circulate and get to the walls through vertical conduits, parts of which are still visible). The western *caldarium,* which is also the largest, had three marble cisterns, and the other rooms had mosaic floors. When the site was renovated after the Visigoth invasion, the large heated chambers were divided into smaller unconnected rooms. The building was decorated with a colonnade along two of its sides (only the foundations of the columns have survived) and with several sculptures, a few pieces of which were found on the very spot where they had been stacked away after the destruction of A.D. 395.

The **theatre** of Argos lies due west of the baths, on the slopes of Larissa. It was constructed at the end of the 4th or the beginning of the 3rd century B.C. and remodelled twice during the Roman era (during the 2nd and the 4th centuries A.D., at which time the orchestra was converted into a cistern and used for

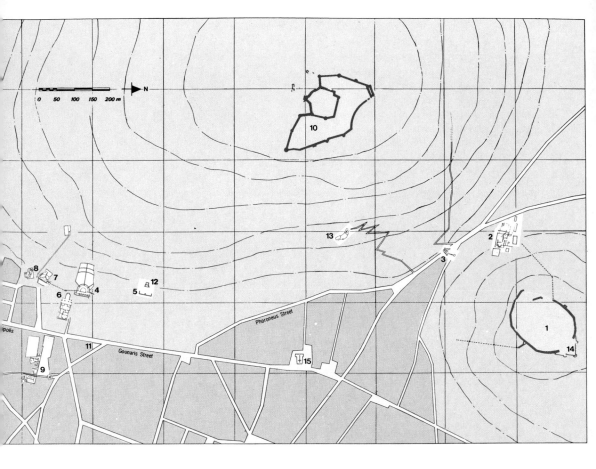

## Plan of Argos

1. Aspis
2. Sanctuaries
   of Pythian Apollo and
   of Athena the Sagacious
3. Mycenaean tombs

4. Theatre
5. Kriterion
6. Thermae
7. Odeum
8. Sanctuary of Aphrodite
9. Agora

10. Larissa
11. House of the mosaics
12. Cistern
13. Panaghia tou Vrachou
14. Bastion
15. St. John

nautical games). Of the Greek *skene* (scene) or stage building (*proscenium,* background structure, and Doric stoa on its outer side) only the foundations remain; they are visible today because the ruins of the Roman mud brick remodelling were intentionally removed during the excavations. Right beneath the skene, an underground passage (the so-called *charoneam steps*) led to the *orchestra* which was circular, had a 26 m. diameter, and a *thymele* (altar) in the middle. There were two *parodoi,* or passageways, between the skene and the auditorium; the southern *parodos* is decorated with reliefs of the Dioscuri. In the *orchestra* there is a base (there were two originally) dating from the time of the Emperor Gratian (375-383). The first row of seats was of marble and was reserved for the dignitaries; in the *koilon* of the seats of the auditorium were carved into the rock 81 rows of seats divided vertically into six asymmetrical

41. *The impressive remains of the Roman baths erected in the 2nd century A.D., south of the agora at Argos.*

sections and horizontally into two tiers. Originally, the first 60 rows extended to the right and the left of the auditorium forming two additional side sectors built on an artificial fill; thus the total capacity of the Argos theater came to 20,000 spectators, the largest number that any Greek theater could hold.

A little further south there is a similar structure, the **odeum,** or theater for musical performances. Thirty-five rectilinear rows of seats have survived, each one about 30 m. long; they are divided into two sections and are carved into the rock. From as early as the 5th century B.C. the citizens of Argos used this site for their assemblies. A small semi-circular theater built in the 1st century and remodelled in the 3rd century A.D. seems to have covered up the earlier seats completely. It was used for musical performances or, possibly, for the same purpose as the earlier one, i.e. as an assembly hall. The first 14 rows that have survived are divided into two sections, just as the original auditorium. The seats rested on a radial substructure. The mosaic floors of the *orchestra* (9.50 m. diameter) and of the *parodoi* suggest that the theater was roofed. The *pros-*

*42. The theatre of Argos, west of the baths, on the slopes of Larissa hill. The tiers of seats (kerkides) can be seen, as well as, the orchestra and the ruins of the skene (scene).*

*cenium* (present height 0.70 m.) is decorated with a series of niches initially faced with marble. Of the *skene* only the foundations are visible.

About 50 m. south of the odeum, the **sanctuary of Aphrodite** was found on a level clearing at the bottom of the rock. It consists of a temple within a poros stone enclosure (only a portion of it can be seen), a portico and a staircase. In the rear, on an artificial platform partly hewn into the rock and partly supported by a retaining wall, stood the temple, built in 430-420 B.C. and destroyed by the Visigoths. It measured 13.40 × 6.20 m., consisted of a *pronaos* and a sanctuary, and rested on a triple platform which is preserved almost intact. Nothing of the superstructure remains. In front of the temple was the altar (6 m. long and 1.75 m. wide) of which only the core has survived. The facing has gone. Pausanias tells us that in front of the temple stood a relief of Telesilla, the heroic poetess of Argos.

North-east of the theater, on the footpath leading up to Larissa, there is an artificial level clearing (35 × 21 m.) reinforced with a strong polygonal and probably Archaic terrace wall. In the middle of it there used to be a staircase that led to the platform where one can still see the remains of a small quadrangular enclosure. The terrace wall had built-in reliefs of three deities — the *Epitelides*, godesses of vengeance. Because of this and because of its similarity to the Areopagus in Athens, the site became known as the **kriterion** (court of justice) where, according to Pausanias, Danaos brought his daughter Hypermestra to trial for having disobeyed him and refused to kill her husband Lynkeus. Behind and above the level clearing, the Romans built a vaulted cistern with arches (**nymphaeum**); the **aqueduct** built during Hadrian's time, still visible on the hill-side, stretched between this cistern and the church of the **Hidden Virgin** or **Virgin of the Rocks** (formerly a monastery) built during the Turkish occupation on top of a cave, probably the site of the ancient sanctuary of *Hera Akraia*. A miraculous icon of the Virgin was found in the crypts of the church. From here a road with several gradations comes down to the Deiras pass; on its eastern side, i.e. at the south-western foot-hills of Aspis, one can still see some Mycenaean tombs of the 14th and 13th centuries B.C.

Just above the cemetery, on the western foot-hills of Aspis, stood the sanc-tuary of **Pythian Apollo** (also called Apollo Deiradiotes, from Deiras) and of **Athena the Sagacious;** it was erected in the 5th century B.C., but later a church and other early Christian and Byzantine structures, belonging to the 5th and the 10th centuries A.D. were built over it so that the ancient monuments have either disappeared completely or are almost unidentifiable, since all that remains are some foundation layers and some rock cuttings. As the terrain is uphill and rugged, the buildings of the sanctuary were erected on four artificial terraces. On the lowest (western) terrace, a stepped altar with rungs cut into the rock (its facing has disappeared) and markings from the bases of votive offerings and of tripods have survived. Northwards, to the left, there used to be a long and narrow two-storey building with a stoa, perhaps a propylon and, behind the altar, a monumental ten-step, 27 m. wide staircase leading to the second terrace. Here stood the temple (destroyed when the church was built) and, on its north side, a quadrilateral structure built of mud brick over a stone lower masonry course, presumably the site of the oracle. To the east, there are two more terraces each on a different level: on the northern one, one can still see the contours of a square building which was later destroyed to make way for a hypostyle cistern; on the southern there are ruins of a circular structure, also destroyed and badly gutted in the middle. One of these structures must have been the temple of Athena.

The footpath which starts from Deiras and leads to the sanctuary continues up to the top of Aspis and winds up at the chapel of **Aghios Elias.** The chapel is built on the site of a settlement of the late Middle Helladic period. Some time later (the exact date is not known) a polygonal wall was built, forming a small citadel (at some points the wall rests on Cyclopean foundations, assumed to be the ruins of Mycenaean fortifications). During the Hellenistic period two towers were added on the points where the city's wall joined the earlier fortifications. These fortifications were repaired and completed at different times by the Byzantines and the Venetians, who also added a new wall around the original one with three bastions on the north side. Inside the fortifications, walls from Hellenistic houses, the foundations of an Archaic temple and an underground cistern, indicate that the area had been continuously inhabited.

Three roads lead to the top of **Larissa:** a steep track on the east slope; a more accessible footpath starting above the theater, by the church of Aghios Georgios and the town's water cistern (a 45 min. climb); and a motor-way starting at

*43. The church of the Hidden Virgin on the slopes of Larissa hill built on top of a cave.*

Deiras and meeting the footpath up at the citadel, right above the modern monastery of Agia Marina.

There are two lines of fortifications — the inner and the outer — built in the 10th century A.D. and incorporating some sections of the 6th and 5th century B.C. polygonal walls (mainly visible on the northern and north-eastern sides) and another small section of what looks like a Cyclopean wall. The fortifications were completed by the Frankish rulers of Argos who added towers at the corners, by the Venetians who constructed the southern and south-western bastions, and by the Turks. The outer ellipsoid wall surrounds the inner hexagonal citadel. Here the poros stone foundations of two temples were found; according to Pausanias, the temples were dedicated to the Larissian Zeus and to Pallas Athena. Today only part of the stepped platform of one of them is visible, but it is not known which one it was.

*44. Ruins of the temple of the goddess Hera at the Heraion of Argos. 5th century B.C.*

# THE HERAION

The Heraion — the sanctuary of Hera, patron goddess of Argos — lies at the southern foot-hills of the Aetovouno (Euboea) range, the summit of which was called Akraia in ancient times. One hour's walking distance from Mycenae (remains of the old Mycenaean road are still visible at some points) and two hours (8 km.) from Argos, the sanctuary was built on two originally smooth level clearings flanked on the right and the left by waterfalls, by the Castro Ravine on the west side (the ancient Elephtherion) and the Glykeia on the east side (ancient Asterion). The area was inhabited from as early as 3000 B.C., but the earliest identified settlement dates from Mycenaean times (15th-13th centuries B.C.). The tholos tomb discovered at Asprochoma, 700 m. north-west of the site, and the chamber tombs found on the slopes of Gerogalaro, off the Castro Ravine, belong to this period. The Geometric era has left no vestiges. The oldest struc- ture of the sanctuary, the old temple, was built at the end of that era and at the beginning of the 7th century B.C. The sanctuary flourished mainly in the 5th century B.C., but continued to prosper well into the Roman era, as is evident from Pausanias's description of it, in the 2nd century A.D. Its importance to the entire Argolid was very great. Besides being the site of annual festivals, the sanctuary was also used to celebrate the official ending of the Heraia Games (archery contests held at Argos in the second year after each Olympiad). In addition, official chronology for Argos was determined from the name of the Hera priestess and the year of her tenure.

The site was first discovered by General Gordon in 1831 and was later explored by Bursian and Rangavis (1854), by Schliemann (1874) and by Stamatakis, who unearthed the tholos tomb (1878). More thorough excavations, however, were undertaken by the American School of Classical Studies in 1892-1895 (Waldstein) and in 1925-1928 (by Blegen who explored the Mycenaean cemetery). Most recent research (1947-49) by the American and the French Schools of Archaelogy (Caskey-Amandry) focused on a study of the stratigraphy of the place.

Nothing has survived of the buildings beyond the foundations, or at the most the first or second courses of the walls, so that the visitor will find it difficult to visualize their ancient splendour. However, the careful study of their remains made a fairly accurate reproduction of their original form possible.

Upon entering the site, the visitor finds himself before an incline strewn with the remains of a large, stepped, poros stone embankment, originally measuring 81 m. wide, which on the right hand side (east) terminates in a strong downhill

45. *Reconstruction of the buldings at the Argive Heraion, including the late 5th century temple.*

retaining wall. The steps are wide enough to serve as a staircase, but its main function was to serve as a terrace wall to retain the earth of the slope; it was also used as a vantage point by those who wished to watch the procession arriving from Argos. The procession was headed by 100 sacrificial cattle, followed by the chariot of Hera's priestess drawn by two cows. (According to legend, when once the priestess Kydippe had to visit the Heraion and the sacred cows were no-where to be found, her sons Cleobis and Biton yoked themselves to the chariot and pulled it to the sanctuary. Their mother asked the goddess to reward their piety and filial devotion, and the goddess granted them the favour of dying happily in their sleep.) The right hand section of the steps goes up to the artificial platform which supported the **classical temple**; at its top there is a small square foundation, probably the altar. On the left side, the steps went to about half-way up only. Above them there was a long, narrow **Doric stoa** with an interior colonnade. Its rear touches the retaining wall of the temple's platform with which it is contemporary. Platform, stoa, and the stepped embankment were all built in about the middle of the 5th century B.C.

The footpath up to the sanctuary curves smoothly to the left (westwards) and goes by a large square building with a peristyle court in the middle; it existed already before the temple's platform was built and belongs to the end of the 6th century B.C. (some scholars place it in the 5th century B.C.). The entrance was on the north side of the building where there were three rooms, each of which had eleven pedestals along the walls for couches with built-in tables in front of them. It was obviously a **banqueting hall** where official symposia were probably held after the festivals.

Behind and slightly above the banqueting hall, there is another **stoa** built, like the southern one, in the 5th century B.C.; It has a wide terrace in front of its facade. All that survives today is the rear foundation of the stoa, the middle wall on which the pillars of the inner colonnade rested, and the retaining wall which supported the frontal terrace. Proceeding between the two buildings and continuing eastwards, one reaches the platform on which the temple was built, exactly on top of the Mycenaean settlement. The strong retaining wall which supported it had an ashlar façade built of well-cut stone blocks. It has been preserved, only partly, thus exposing the less carefully built core.

In the middle of the platform there is the later **temple of Hera,** built in 420 B.C. by the Argive architect Eupolemos; it has an east-west axis, with an entrance on its east side. The interior of its cella has been excavated as deep as the Mycenaean stratum. Only its triple stepped platform (39.50 × 20 m.) and the entrance ramp on the east side have been preserved, but fragments and information handed down by the ancient Greeks enable us to reconstruct the temple quite accurately: it was a Doric structure with 6 columns on the façades and 12 on the sides; the columns (7.40 m. high) were hewn of local stone and coated with white plaster. The roof tiles were of marble and so were the sculptures decorating the cornice. The eastern pediment depicted the Birth of Zeus, the western pediment the Fall of Troy and the metopes were decorated with scenes from the Battle of the Gods against the Giants (Gigantomachy) and from the Battle of the Greeks against the Amazons (Amazonomachy). Its proportions and some of the morphological details indicate a strong Attic influence. In front of the entrance stood statues of heroes and of priestesses of Hera. In the front porch were statues of the Graces, Hera's bed (probably a ceremonial object), and a shield which, according to legend, Menelaus had captured in Troy after slaying Euphorbus. The cella was divided into three aisles by interior

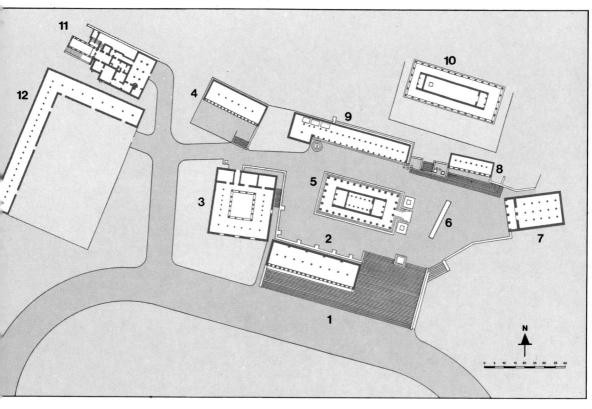

## Plan of the Argive Heraion

1. Staircase
2. Stoa
3. Banqueting house
4. Stoa
5. Temple of Hera
6. Altar
7. Square hypostyle structure
8. Stoa
9. Stoa
10. Temple of Hera (old)
11. Baths
12. Gymnasium

colonnades. In the center there was a gold and ivory seated statue of Hera by Polycleitus, and a very old idol of Hera made of wild pear-tree wood, which the Argives had seized in Tiryns in 468 B.C. The temple and the area around it contained many other valuable offerings of all periods.

In front of the temple, at an angle, a particularly long and narrow **altar** (17 × 2.40 m.) was built during the Hellenistic period. Further to the east, on an extension of the terrace, there is a square hypostyle structure measuring 28.90 ×17.10 m. (possibly a ceremonial edifice) with a western hall and a triple internal colonnade, constructed of poros stone, built in the middle of the 5th century B.C. at the same time as the platform and the stoas, somewhat earlier than the temple.

North of the temple lies the earlier complex of buildings which, along with the banqueting hall, belonged to the *old temple*. The upper levelling of the slope was reshaped into a platform measuring 56×34 m., some of it cut into the rock and some of it reinforced by an enormous Cyclopean terrace wall which is visible from quite a distance. At the foot of the wall, there are ruins of two buildings dating from the end of the 7th or the beginning of the 6th century B.C.

*46. The Heraion of Argos. The temple of Hera can be seen, as well as, the ruins of a doric stoa of the 6th century B.C.*

The right hand side (eastern) building is a small **stoa** with an internal colonnade, similar in arrangement to the southern stoa lower down (even to the stepped incline in front of it). Some time in later years two transversal walls were built (their foundations can still be seen) dividing the interior into three parts. The façade was also probably blocked up. Next to it, on the western side, there is another longer **stoa** (63×10.50 m.) also with an internal colonnade, and a closed, slightly projecting wing on its western extremity. Three cisterns of a later period were found in the interior of this stoa.

A passageway (probably with gradations) between the two stoas led to the upper level of the **old temple,** (early 7th century B.C.), which was burnt down due to the carelessness of the priestess Chryseis in 423 B.C. The temple was 47 m. long and 19 m. wide, but only a section of the southern stylobate is preserved, parts of the wall of the cella, and the square pedestal of the statue. The walls, were made of brick and the original roof was certainly thatched as is evidenced by a contemporary clay model of a building, found at the Heraion.

*47. Reconstruction of the later temple of Hera, with her chryselephantine statue. The goddess originally held a sceptre in her left hand and a pomegranate in her right.*

Later on, in the middle of the 7th century B.C., a wooden colonnade resting on round stone bases (0.50 m. diameter) was added around the temple and the new roof was covered with brick tiles.

The decision to replace the old monument seems to have been taken even before it was destroyed by fire; thus the terrace for the new temple had already been built and so had the southern stoa and the eastern hypostyle building. After the construction of the new temple, the sanctuary was left unchanged except for the addition of the Hellenistic altar. Later, during the Roman Imperial period, two more structures were built on the western side of the hill, on the banks of the waterfall: a **public bath** with an underground heating system on the southern side, a porch with a mosaic floor on the eastern side, and a cistern on the western side; and to the south, a **gymnasium** measuring 34×34 m. flanked by stoas to the north and west. The two structures were evidently meant for visitors to the sanctuary, but they are built at some distance and do not form an organic part of the whole complex.

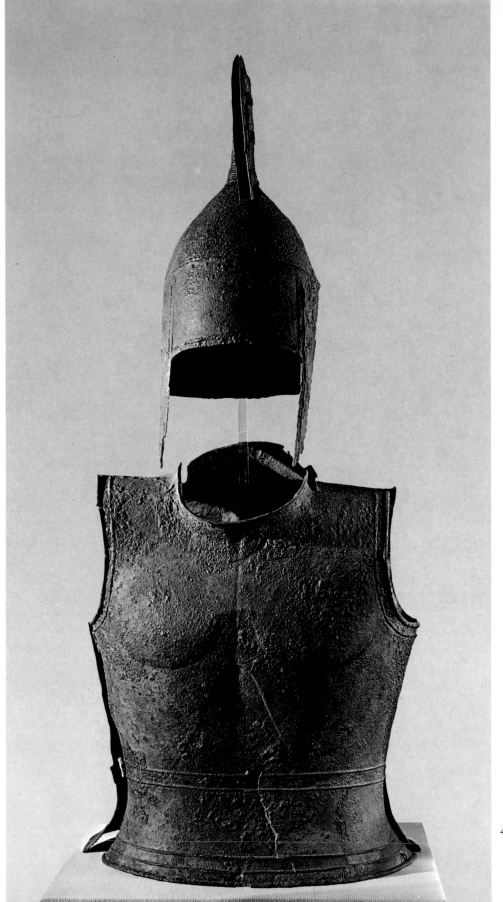

48

# THE MUSEUM OF ARGOS

The museum is housed in a new building on Olga Street (a gift of the French School of Archaeology) which has been connected to the older (Neoclassical) Kallergis mansion.

The Argos finds are exhibited on the *first floor* of the building, to the right of the entrance; large, Middle and Late Helladic jars stand in the hall, while other items are placed in glass cases in chronological order from the entrance to the rear. The first cases on both sides of the room contain Middle Helladic and Mycenaean objects, mainly vases, most of them found in the Deiras graves. The next cases contain Proto-Geometric, Geometric and Late-Geometric exhibits; at the rear, four built-in glass cases contain, among other things, an Archaic tortoise shell lyre and a vase depicting the blinding of Polyphemus by Odysseus and his companions. Other objects worth noting are the iron boat-shaped Geometric spit-stands (case no. **8**), the spits (case no. **9**), and in the middle of the room the Late-Geometric bronze helmet and breast-plate of an Argive warrior.

*The second floor* contains Roman sculpture — statues (most of them copies of Classical originals such as the Farnese Hercules and the statue of Corinna), busts and reliefs, as well as a mosaic with a simple decorative design. The basement of the Kallergis mansion contains the Lerna finds; these are mostly pottery, also arranged in chronological order from left to right of the entrance (Neolithic, Early Helladic, Middle Helladic, Late Helladic). In the middle of the room we can see a restored and completed circular Early Helladic clay hearth. In a special case to the left there is a Neolithic clay idol of a woman and in the case at the rear of the room a fine square roof tile from the House of Tiles.

In the Museum courtyard there are several architectural pieces and sculptures from various parts of Argos and the surrounding area. *The mosaics* (seasons and months of the year, Dionysos and his companions) found in the post-Roman house near the theater (see above) are kept in sheds on the left hand side of the courtyard.

48. *Bronze breastplate and helmet, found in a late Geometric grave at Argos. The breastplate is bell-shaped; the helmet consists of a cone covering the brow and the nape of the neck, two cheek-pieces and a tall crest shaped like a horse-shoe. 7th century B.C.*

*49. Terracotta figurine of a kourotrophos (nursing mother) of Type Φ. The arms and hands that hold the baby are rendered with striking plasticity. 13th century B.C.*

*50. Large geometric krater, one of the finest specimens of Argive pottery. It is decorated with meanders, lines, birds and two antithetical male figures, each holding a horse. 8th century B.C.*

*51. Geometric vase with vertical handles. The painted decoration consists of antithetically placed animals within a border and on the left side of the vase, three female dancers. 8th century B.C.*

53

54

52. Large tripod base, exquisitely decorated with linear motifs, meanders, birds and animals arranged in contrasting patterns. Below the handles there are figures of wrestlers, which may have had mythological or epic connotations. 8th century B.C.

53. Fragment of a large krater with painted decoration consisting of three female dancers holding boughs, surrounded by a border. 8th century B.C.

54. Fragment of a clay krater of the 7th century B.C., depicting Cyclop Polyphemus in a reclining position on the rocky floor of the cave (represented by conventional symbols); standing some distance away, Odysseus, with the help of one of his companions, plunges a long, sharpened pole into the giant's eye.

55

55. *The mosaic of the Months. A Roman mosaic representing the months of March and April personified as men; March is a warrior, April a shepherd. March carries a small flag in his left hand and a dove in his right. A cauldron stands on the ground. April is shown holding a lamb.*

56. *Roman mosaic representing the months of May and June, personified as men, each holding the products typical of the season to which they belong.*

*57. The entrance passage and main gate of the acropolis of Tiryns, leading to the palace.*

# TIRYNS

The citadel of Tiryns, 1.5 km. from the sea, was built on an isolated rocky hill, oblong in shape, rising just over 18 m. above the plain that surrounds it. Its top, extending over about 20,000 sq.m., is relatively smooth. The ancient Greeks believed that its walls had been built by Proitos who had brought in special masons, the Cyclopes, from Lycia. Proitos's brother, Akrisios, was king of Argos and grandfather of Perseus, the founder of Mycenae. Thus, tradition accepted that Tiryns had been fortified two generations before Mycenae — a belief which coincides with the findings of the archaeologists. One of Perseus's descendants was Heracles; and his exiled descendants, never forgetting their Argive origin, eventually managed to return to their homeland. The myths of the Trojan cycle consider Tiryns, Argos, and the whole of Hermionis as belonging to the kingdom of Diomedes, one of the most famous and powerful heroes of the Achaeans. But this is the last we ever hear of Tiryns. Indeed, modern research has shown that at the end of the Mycenaean period the entire citadel was destroyed by fire and that it was abandoned. On its ruins the Geometric temple of Hera was built and the area has been continuously inhabited ever since, although its old glory was lost for ever.

Excavation of the site was begun by Schliemann in 1876, who went back to it in 1884 accompanied by Dörpfeld. After that, excavation was undertaken by the German Archaeological Institute which continues work in the area to this day. It is now known that the hill had been inhabited since Neolithic times. The first buildings (houses of an Early Helladic village built around a large circular structure) go back to about 2500 B.C., but the oldest fortification which encircled the top of the hill, the so-called *Upper Citadel,* was not built until after 1400 B.C. A century later, the east entrance was remodelled, the south wall was reinforced and a rather large area, the *Middle Citadel,* was added to the north side. It took its final form a little before 1200 B.C., when the east entrance was made truly impregnable, the curved wall of the west bastion was added on the opposite side, the south wall was broadened and the Middle Citadel was further strengthened by adding the long and narrow fortifications of the *Lower Citadel* which encompassed the remaining surface of the hill and ensured the fortress's water supply. This then is how Tiryns looks today; it consists of the Cyclopean fortifications that encircle it, the late 13th century B.C. palace complex, and the Lower Citadel area, most of it still unexcavated.

The main approach to the acropolis is on the eastern, inland side of the hill. It begins with a huge **Cyclopean ramp,** 4.70 m. wide, and originally much longer than the restored part we see today. At the end of the ramp one turns right, goes through an open *passageway* which used to be as wide as the ramp (the two low

58. *Aerial view of the acropolis of Tiryns, showing the Cyclopean fortifications.*
*The citadel was built on a small hill in the Argive plain.*

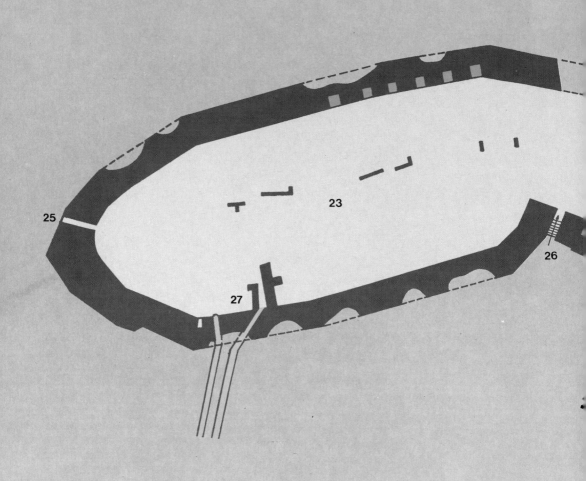

## Plan of the citadel of Tiryns

1. Cyclopean ramp
2. Passage
3. Main gate
4. Gate (earlier entrance)
5. Courtyard
6. Galleries
7. Great propylon
8. Outer courtyard of the palace
9. Gallery
10. Guard house? Archives room?
11. Propylon
12. Central courtyard of the palace
13. Great Megaron
14. Bathroom

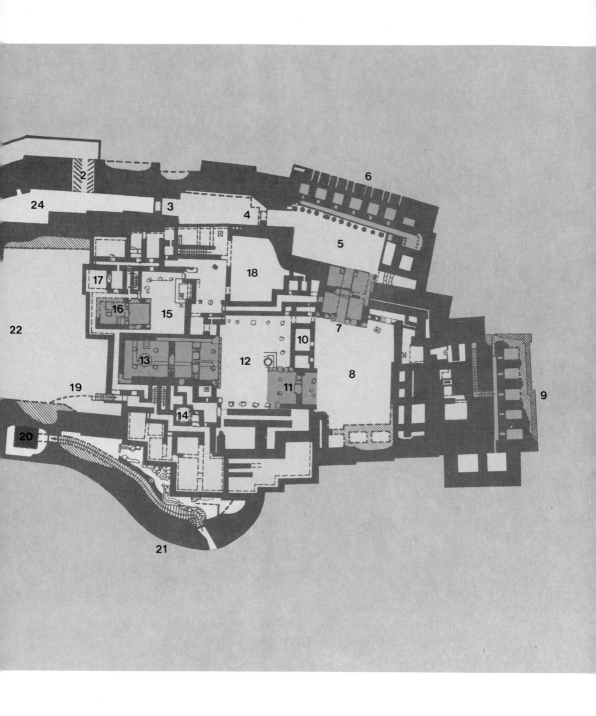

walls on either side of it were built at a later period) and on to a narrow passage between the outer wall (3rd period) and the inner wall (2nd period). The passage leads to the Lower Citadel, to the north, and to the **main gate** of the acropolis, to the south — in shape, dimensions and arrangement very similar to the Lion Gate at Mycenae. Today only the jambs are preserved, at about half their original height, and the threshold with the cylindrical pivot holes for the hinges of the wooden door panels. The jambs had two horizontal holes for the heavy wooden bolt (the east hole, which is the point where the jamb now ends, continues well into the thickness of the wall). After the gate, the passage widens a little, goes through another *gate* (the earlier entrance of the second period which was retained in the third period as a supplementary gate) of which only a few stones of the treshold's substructure have survived, and ends in an open courtyard; along the left (east) side of this courtyard, one can see the bases of a colonnade which belonged to a long and narrow **stoa** opening on to the court. A little further on one follows an improvised modern downhill path and reaches a long and narrow corridor, only 1.65 m. wide, with a corbel roof — one of the famous vaulted galleries of Tiryns; **the gallery** runs under the stoa, through the wall (11 m. thick in that part), and communicates with a series of square store-rooms measuring 4.30 × 3.30 m., also with corbel roofs. The vaulted gallery had long remained open, and for centuries had served as a shelter to the flocks of the area who gave the stones a particular polish as they huddled together and rubbed against them.

The west side of the court is flanked by the **great propylon** of the palace of which we can see only the threshold, the lower stone courses of the walls, the bases of the jambs which still bear the marks of the saw that cut them into the desired shape and the holes into which the beams of the panelling were fast-ened. The propylon consists of an inner and an outer stoa with jambs at the edges of their side walls and two columns on the façade. The two stoas were separated by a transversal wall with a door whose opening in the middle (3.17 m.) corresponded with the distance between the two façade columns. In the north wall of the inner stoa there was a small side door from which a corridor led directly to the inner apartments of the palace. Through this majestic propylon one comes to the **outer courtyard**, an irregular rectangle in shape, originally paved with plaster. Its south side is flanked by the south fortification wall, built at different periods. The successive additions, enlargements and remodellings have resulted in a complex uneven structure, 17 m. thick, with various rooms built in its interior, probably for storage purposes. The most characteristic of these additions are certainly those made during the last period. They consist of an inner **vaulted gallery** with rooms, similar to those found under the entrance courtyard, which can be reached by a staircase originally intended to lead out to a small gate in the wall but subsequently sealed by the wall of the gallery. At the east end of the vaulted gallery there was a wide opening whose sides narrowed outward into a kind of loophole. On the ruins of the inner section of the wall, on the north side of the court, a small **Byzantine church** had been built, around which there were several shallow graves. Its foundations, as well as a threshing-floor which had covered them up later, were removed during excavations.

The north side of the court is flanked by two rooms (perhaps a guard-house or archives room) and a **second propylon,** similar in arrangement to the first one but smaller, with a 2.95 m. opening in the middle and a two-panel door. From here one reached the **central courtyard** of the palace which was almost square (17.75 × 20.25 m.), and had a plaster floor. Near the right inner jamb of the

59. *One of the best pre-
served galleries in the
acropolis of Tiryns. The
upper courses of the
walls are corbelled in-
wards, narrowing to a
sharp angle at the top.*

60. *The ramp on the east
side of the acropolis,
leading to the main en-
trance.*

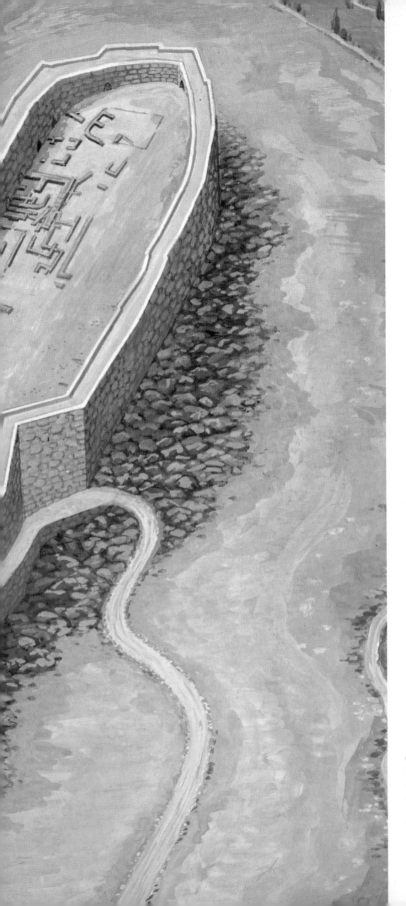

*61. Reconstruction of the Acropolis at Tiryns, showing the Upper, Middle and Lower citadel, as well as the great and small megaron and the western bastion.*

*62. The palace on the acropolis of Tiryns: detail of the megaron. The columns bases of an open stoa are still in situ.*

propylon there was a round low structure, most probably a sacrificial pit, remodelled into a square shape in post-Mycenaean times. The north side of the courtyard is almost entirely occupied by the **great megaron** of the palace. Its façade consists of a porch (9.65 × 4.80 m.), an open stoa with two columns between its end jambs (the bases are still *in situ*) and a floor which is raised above the level of the courtyard by two steps. The lower course of the west wall had a decorative band of alabaster slabs with relief sculptures inlaid with pieces of lapis lazuli (National Archaeological Museum of Athens). The two-panel doors, 1.72 m. wide, lead from the chamber to the vestibule. The vestibule (9.70 × 4.72 m.) has a small side door which communicates with the apartments west of the megaron, and another large central door without panels which leads to the main hall of the megaron, the domos (9.75-9.86×11.81 m.). At its center there was a round hearth, 3.30 m. in diameter, flanked by four equidistant wooden pillars of which the stone bases have survived. By the east wall, in front of the hearth, there was a low quadrilateral dais upon which rested the king's throne. The floor was paved with stucco depicting octopi and dolphins painted within square frames.

Today the width of the megaron is divided into two by a relatively narrow wall built of different materials, which turns shortly before reaching to the back wall of the domos, thus creating a rectangular space almost like the east half of

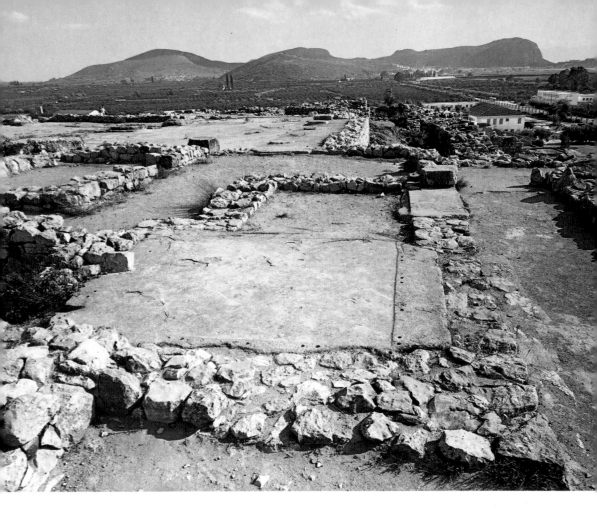

*63. The palace of Tiryns: The bathroom floor, consisting of an enormous limestone slab. At the north-eastern corner a conduit carried the water to a T-shaped light-shaft.*

the megaron; it rests partly on the floor and partly on the rubble base of the eastern wall. It is, in other words, a later construction, the temple of Hera erected in Geometric times and built over the debris of the megaron; some smaller, humbler houses were built in different parts of the citadel during the same period.

A distinctive feature of the apartments between the megaron and the west wall is that they all communicated with the courtyard, the vestibule of the megaron, and the west entrance to the citadel (see below). Also that they were built with special care and were decorated with frescoes. Evidently these were the royal apartments which also included a **bathroom** — a small square room with an enormous 20-ton stone slab for a floor. The slab is framed by a slightly projective band carved with small square holes to accommodate the wide vertical boards that panelled the walls; at the north-eastern corner a conduit carried the water to an adjacent T-shaped *light-shaft* and a drain. At the north side of the light-shaft there used to be a staircase, which means that there was at least one more storey on the west wing of the palace.

The megaron, the bathroom, the light-shaft and the staircase are separated from the other west rooms by a corridor, a branch of which continues behind the megaron and meets, east of it, a second smaller *courtyard* (9.20×18.45 m.) with a stoa on its east side; later a small square room was added to the south corner of the stoa. On the north side, one step above ground level, lies the **small mega-ron.** It consists of a deep square porch (5.05 × 5.59 m.) with a narrow and therefore columnless façade, two side doors giving onto the corridor which encircles it, and a larger central door giving onto the domos. The domos, measuring 5.64×7.60 m., was also columnless; its floor was divided into squares painted with abstract decorative motifs; there was a square hearth in the middle and to its right, by the east wall, vestiges of the dais of a throne were found, just as in the great megaron. At the south-west corner, a square mud brick partition was built at the end of the Mycenaean period.

At the north-west corner of the courtyard, to the right of the small megaron, there was a staircase behind which there was a *megaron-type* apartment consist-ing of two connecting rooms, an antechamber and a domos, with entrances on either side of the antechamber. East of these apartments and of the courtyard, there is another courtyard, a series of rooms (workshops or store-rooms), and still another staircase.The entire wing, in other words, had a second floor. The first excavators thought that this wing was reserved for the female members of the royal family or for the crown prince; but it later became apparent that it was built at an earlier stage, before the palace had been extended to the west covering the entire area of the Upper Citadel, and before the great megaron and its courtyard had been built.

Between the east wing, the courtyard of the great megaron, the outer propy-lon and the entrance to the acropolis, there is a large area full of bits of walls with no clear plan, described by the excavators as *"remains of houses."*

Returning to the corridor behind the north-west corner of the great megaron we come upon a gradated downhill path toward the fortification wall, which develops further down into a flagstone passageway. The end of this passage has not been preserved so that the visitor has now to go around it and to follow a somewhat rough path downhill which takes him over the section of the enceinte that has been preserved and to the steps of the west gate of the acropolis. This small auxiliary entrance, which faces the sea, was added during the last phase of the building of the fortifications and is extremely well designed and finely constructed. At the west wall of the *Middle Citadel* where the flag-stone pas-sageway ended, a square tower had been erected around a steep crevice forming a natural pit over which no permanent construction was ever built. By the downhill side of the tower a strong curving wall was built — the **western bastion,** which skirted the earlier indented fortification wall and cut across a path that climbed up to the tower. The path was replaced by a wide stone stairway built into the interior of the bastion (the first 65 steps have survived); the stairway began at the small west gate, was 1.50 m. wide, and rose obliquely to the wall forming a loophole protected by a corbel vault, whose interior opening was much wider that its exterior one; it had no door and could therefore never close. This arrangement limited the number of attackers to a minimum while it allowed a small party of defenders to confront any number of agressors. Those of the enemy who did manage to get through, had to climb the stairs between the two lines of fortifications (the inner and the outer) while being hit from all sides. And even if they were able to reach the tower, the open pit — which would normally have been covered with a wooden bridge — checked their advance for good.

The Middle Citadel, although also inhabited, was never thoroughly investi-gated and its remains which, among other things, included a potter's kiln, were covered up even before the findings were published.

Almost the same thing happened in the case of the Lower Citadel where research began only recently and the excavated area is therefore not open to visitors. By walling it, the entire extent of the rocky eminence, which until then had been unfortified, was added to the citadel and at the same time ensured its water supply, just as at Mycenae.

The main approach to the *Lower Citadel* is from the east, by a narrow passage reached by the ramp of the entrance. Here the visitor turns right, northwards, and walks between the old wall of the second period and the newer section of the third period, which forms the beginning of the fortifications of the Lower Citadel. About 12 m. beyond the gate, on the inner façade of this wall, there is a high vaulted niche which, in all probability was a gate shrine. Further down, at various points of the wall, there is a series of large square niches probably used for storage, some of which had already been blocked in the Mycenaean period. There are also two secondary small arched gates: one at the north corner, high up on the wall like a large window; the other in the south-west corner near the wall of the Middle Citadel, has steps, a threshold, and a single panelled door. But the most important discovery were two adjacent openings, also vaulted, at the north-western corner; they go through the entire thickness of the wall and continue into two parallel underground **galleries** about 20 m. long, dug deep into the ground; they served as cisterns, where water was collected from the surrounding area. All of the areas excavated in the Lower Citadel, and especially those in front of the entrance to the galleries, revealed the foundations of buildings of various periods which indicate that the rock of Tiryns, whether walled or un-walled, had been inhabited during the entire period of the Bronze Age.

The surrounding area was also inhabited. At the eastern, south-eastern and southern foot of the hill some houses were found belonging to various periods of the Mycenaean era. The earliest of these houses is contemporary to the first building phase of the citadel (14th century B.C.); the latest, a large *megaron-type* structure (beneath the eastern gallery, at the turning of the asphalt road going to the entrance of the archaeological site), was built after the last phase and continued to be inhabited long after the destruction of the citadel. There are similar ruins and some tombs on the other side of the hill, in front of the western bastion.

Two more constructions belong to the Tiryns settlement, although these are outside the immediate area of the citadel. A **tholos tomb** was discovered about 1 km. to the east, at the western foot-hills of the high conical hill of Prophet Elias; it is accessible by the asphalt road leading from the archaelogical site eastwards to Kofini (New Tiryns). The tomb, found whole and in perfect condition, is a corbelled structure built of untrimmed slabs, of a much simpler construction than that of the later luxurious tholos tombs of Mycenae. The tomb had been completely despoiled ever since Roman times, when an olive-press was installed in the tholos. Some chamber tombs were also found in the area.

Four kilometers east of the acropolis, just before reaching the village of Aghios Adrianos (Katsigri), there are three watercourses which, in ancient times, used to flood the Tiryns area quite frequently. In the Mycenaean period an earth dam reinforced with Cyclopean masonry, was built at their confluence to check the flow and channel the waters through a torrent bed, into a south-bound ravine, away from the citadel. The dam is till visible today, 1¹/₄ km. north of Aghios Adrianos, and is one of the few known technical works of the Mycenaean era.

64

# FINDS FROM TIRYNS
# IN THE NATIONAL ARCHAEOLOGICAL MUSEUM
# OF ATHENS

Finds from the acropolis and the lower city at Tiryns are exhibited in the Mycenaean Room of the National Archaeological Museum in Athens. They include fresco fragments from the palace (figures, almost life size, from a procession of women, and miniature scenes of a wild boar hunt, bull leaping, two women in a chariot, etc.), and a variety of objects ranging from the Protohelladic to the Geometric periods (case 15). Most of them, and certainly the most important, come from a single "treasure"; these are a group of heterogeneous objects from different periods that were collected, and then concealed. It includes bronze daggers and vessels, necklaces with gold beads, a curved sword of iron, wheels made of golden wire and electrum beads from central Europe that belonged to a model of a chariot, and two large rings with elliptical bezels. On one of them is carved one of the best known examples of Mycenaean art — a scene of zoomorphic demons approaching a seated goddess in a ritual fertility procession.

The other has a scene of human figures in front of a building, taking their farewell and embarking on a ship riding at anchor.

*64. Gold ring from the "treasure" of Tiryns. It depicts a scene of leave-taking, with passengers embarking on a Mycenaean ship. The representation is powerful and life-like, especially as regards the movements of the human figures. 14th or 13th century B.C.*

*65. Gold ring with a religious theme from the "treasure" of Tiryns. The goddess is sitting on a folding chair, holding a chalice-shaped cup in her raised hand with a bird behind her and a censer in front of her. Four lion-headed daemons bearing libation vessels are advancing towards the goddess. 15th century B.C.*

66

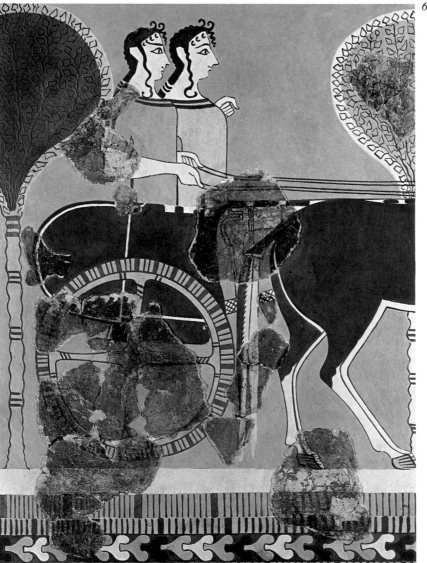

67

66. Fragment of a fre[sco]
from the later palac[e at]
Tiryns, showing a b[oar]
hunt. The hounds ar[e in]
full cry after the b[oar]
which has been stuck [be-]
tween the eyes by [the]
huntsman's javelin. [All]
that remains of [the]
huntsman is one of [his]
hands. 13th century B[.C.]

67. Fresco depic[ting]
two women in a char[iot,]
from the later palac[e at]
Tiryns. 13th cen[tury]
B.C.

68. Fragment of a fre[sco]
depicting a processio[n of]
women, from the l[ater]
palace at Tiryns: [a]
woman's head, with [de-]
tails of the prelimi[nary]
drawing of the face [dis-]
tinctly visible. 13th c[en-]
tury B.C.

# NAUPLIA

Two steep rock formations dominate the eastern seashore of the bay of the Argolid: the rock of Palamidi, 216 m. high, and, at its feet, the rock of Akronauplia, only 85 m. high, which projects into the sea and closes the bay. The two formations are connected by a narrow strip of land. At their northern foot-hills lies the town of Nauplia. Except for some prehistoric finds and the remains of a polygonal wall of the 3rd century B.C. on Akronauplia, there are no ancient ruins in this area of the town. The closest Mycenaean remains (tombs) were found on the north-eastern foot-hills of Palamidi and, further east, at the modern suburb of Pronoia. This is not very strange: the level area where the town is built was, until the end of the 15th century A.D., shallow uninhabited marshland; it was filled as late as 1470 by the Venetians in order to extend the city and to build new housing for the refugees from Halkis which had then been overrun by the Turks. Until a suitable sub-soil had been created, the first houses were built on oak posts. Thus, in Prehistoric times, the Greek and Roman periods, and throughout the Middle Ages, Nauplia consisted only of Akronauplia and of the northern foot-hills of the two elevations.

In ancient times, Nauplia merely served as the harbour of Argos. It was not till the end of the 3rd century B.C. that the top of Akronauplia became fortified. In the Roman period, the town was abandoned. In the 12th century A.D. the Byzantines fortified Akronauplia, building more or less on the ruins of the ancient wall. In 1210 the town fell to the Franks who extended the citadel eastward and finally conceded it to the Venetians (1389) who, in turn, strengthened the fortifications and built the lower town. In 1540 it fell to the Turks, but in 1686 the Venetians recaptured it, added Palamidi to the fortifications and developed the port to such a degree that it became the capital of their eastern possessions under the name of Napoli di Romania. In 1715 the Turks con-

69. *The fortified islet of the Bourdzi, a bright jewel set in the bay of Nauplia, commanding the harbour.*

70. *The hill of Acronauplia, the town of Nauplia and the Bourdzi offshore, as seen from* ▶
*the Palamidi fortress.*

quered it once again. In 1828 it became the capital of the newly-founded Greek State and the seat of Governor Kapodistrias; King Otto, also landed in Nauplia in 1833, but transferred the capital to Athens a year later. Sightseeing in Nauplia, therefore, is limited to the remains of more recent times — of the Middle Ages, the Venetian period, the Turkish occupation, and the post-revolutionary period.

The citadel of **Akronauplia** consists of four successive fortification walls, each one added to the other. The earliest is at the western end of the cape, which is also the highest part of the hill. This is the fortress built by the Byzantines in the 12th and 13th centuries (*Castel dei Greci*) whose walls had incorporated the remains of the ancient fortifications. It comprised the house of the Garrison Commander and two churches, one of which was the Cathedral, converted into a mosque in 1540. Today, the Byzantine buildings are barely preserved and most of them have disappeared under Venetian additions and alterations, such as the barracks on the north side (used as a prison until a few years ago). A little lower down, east of the Byzantine fortress, the Franks built their own citadel (*Castel dei Franchi*) of which only the foundations of the ruler's palace have survived; later on the palace served as the home of the Venetian chief fiscal officer (Camerlengo). At the southern tip of the narrow strip that joins the cape to the land — the modern Arvanitia coast — there used to be a moat that protected the fortress and continued northwards up to a small bay formed by the sea. A wooden drawbridge was thrown across it.

In 1473, the architect Gambello extended the fortifications further east and erected the long and narrow *Castel Toro* which ended in a double semi-circular tower (the modern Hotel Xenia has been built on its site). Gambello also strengthened the partition between the Greek and the Frankish citadels by building a particularly strong wall which has a side entrance on the south side. A vaulted chamber, accessible from the modern circular road, was incorporated into the wall separating the Frankish citadel from the Castel Toro; the chamber is decorated with barely visible frescoes of religious figures (Jesus Christ, the Lamb of God, the Virgin Mary, saints Anthony, James and George) and lay subjects (Byzantine general, the de Brienne and Villehardouin coats of arms) as well as commemorative representations of the 1291 peace agreement between Andronicus Palaiologus and the Frankish rulers. Another fresco depicts the Virgin framed by the coat of arms of the Venetian governor to whom Nauplia had been ceded in 1394 by Theodore Palaiologus, the despot (prince) of Mystra. During the same period, fortifications were built on the small island of Aghioi Theodoroi (*Castel da Mar*, or *Bourtzi* as it is now called) consisting of a high square tower surrounded by a semi-circular fort; the fortified island was joined to Akronauplia by a 450 m. long chain which closed the entrance to the harbour. Later on the Turks sank huge blocks of stone around it to discourage ships from coming near it and built a pier along the chain. After the liberation, the island fortress became the home of the executioner.

Akronauplia took its final shape in the second Venetian period, at which time the earlier fortifications were remodelled and strengthened; in 1706 the quadrilateral *Grimani bastion* (now planted with cypress trees) was added in front of the Castel Toro towers, thus enabling the fortifications to communicate with the walls of the city and the beginning of the western ascent to Palamidi. The ascent,

*71. Entrance to the Palamidi fortress. Over the gate is a relief of the lion of St. Mark, the emblem of Venice.*

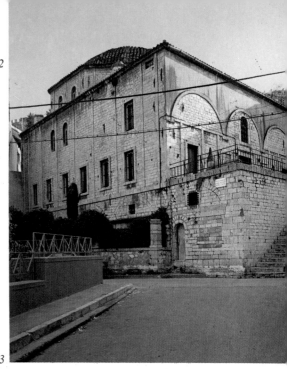

72

73

which is partly covered, consists of 857 steps going up the steep slope of the rock. The western slope is much smoother; it starts in the town itself (25 March Street) and, developing into a motorway, goes as far as the gate of the citadel. **Palamidi** was unfortified and uninhabited until 1711-1714 when the proveditor Sagredo built a fortification designed by LaSalle and Levasseur, the French engineers. Palamidi consists of the Aghios Andreas stronghold (after the chapel next to the western entrance), also called the Garrison Commander's stronghold, and of forts named after Themistocles, Miltiades, Achilles, Phokion, Epaminondas, Leonidas, and Robert; all of these fortifications intercommunicate directly and are connected by a circular wall. The rebelling Greeks overran Palamidi in 1822 and managed to hold on to it until the liberation.

Of the lower city wall only the western section has survived; it starts at the edge of Akronauplia, comes down to the bottom of the rock and follows the coastline up to *Pente Adelphia* (The Five Brothers), a small bastion with five strong guns (4 Venetian cannons and a mortar have been put back into the gun emplacements) built opposite the Bourtzi to block the passage of enemy ships into the harbour.

Walking through the streets of Nauplia, one can visit several monuments of the recent past — Byzantine, Venetian, Turkish, various buildings erected at the time of Kapodistrias and Otto (Turkish fountains, the mansions of the regents Armansberg and Maurer, the first Cadets School, the first Ministry of the Armed Forces, Otto's Gymnasium) and many private neo-Classical houses. Of particular interest are: The **Lion of the Bavarians** at the entrance of the town, a relief sculpted on the rock by Siegel in memory of the Bavarian soldiers who died in the plague epidemic of 1833-34; the church of **Aghios Georgios,** built in 1619 in the Byzantine order, turned into a mosque by the Turks, and, during the second Venetian period, into a Catholic church decorated with frescoes by Italian painters in 1703 (among other things, one can see a copy of Da Vinci's Last Supper); the church of the **Transfiguration of our Saviour,** an old mosque built by the Turks on the site of a Venetian nunnery, subsequently offered to the Catholic community by King Otto; here one notes a wooden arch, a gift of the French philhellene Touret, inscribed with the names of philhellenes who died in the Greek revolution; the church of **Aghios Spyridon** (built in 1702) where Kapodistrias was murdered (the bullet hole on the outer wall near the door is still visible). On the east side of Constitution Square there is a mosque: here Kapodistrias established the **Allilodidaktirion,** one of the first schools that operated after the liberation of Greece. At the south-western edge of the town there is another school, the **Vouleutikon,** so called because this is where the first Parliament of the Hellenes, formed in 1822, used to convene (vouli=parliament). Next to it lies the gloomy Turkish seminary (known as Leonard's prison), today used as storeroom by the Archaeological Museum of Nauplia.

*72. St. Spyridon, the historic church where John Kapodistrias, Governor of Greece, was assassinated. The bullet-hole can still be seen on the site.*

*73. The Vouleutikon, a Turkish mosque used by the Greeks in 1822, during the War of Independence, for meetings of the National Assembly.*

*74. The Venetian naval arsenal, on the west side of Syntagma Square. This building, with its heavy, powerful lines, is regarded as the most representative example of Venetian architecture in Nauplia. It is now the Archaeological Museum.*

75

75. *The Palamidi fortress. This great mass of masonry, with walls and fortifications that made it impregnable, broods menacingly over the town.*

76-77. *The Palamidi fortress. The courtyards of the immence citadel are now deserted, and the later buildingsn which were used as prisons, today lie in ruins.*

77

# THE MUSEUM OF NAUPLIA

The museum itself lies on the west side of the square, in a Venetian building erected in 1713, originally used as a Navy arsenal. The exhibition rooms are on two floors, each consisting of a large rectangular hall with two parallel rows of showcases along each of the longer sides of the room; a number of choice objects are exhibited between the pillars supporting the roof. The objects are arranged in chronological order, starting from the door, then along the length of the right hand wall, the rear wall, and ending at the left hand wall.

The *first floor* contains Prehistoric exhibits. The first showcase to the right contains Neolithic vases from Franchthi and some Early Helladic ones from Asine and Berbati. We then come upon Early Helladic objects from Tiryns (of special interest is an earthenware cooler), and some Middle Helladic pottery, most of it belonging to the earlier Circle B tombs of Mycenae. At the rear of the room we come upon the first Late Helladic exhibits: a palatial style amphora from Circle B, bronzes from the tomb of Midea (note especially the unique bronze panoply, complete with a model helmet made of wild boar's teeth), funerary stelae from Circle B, pottery, Egyptian finds and stone vases from Mycenae, fragments from Tiryns' frescoes, vases from Berbati, Asine and Tiryns (among which a rhyton shaped like the head of a fish) and, finally, the idols and the frescoes from the cult center of Mycenae. On the landing outside the hall, one can see the two stone *Menhirs* from the cenotaph of Midea.

On the *second floor* are exhibited objects of the Historic period. The earliest of these, right in front of the door, is a helmet and objects belonging to a burial found in a sub-Mycenaean tomb at Tiryns. Then come some proto-Geometric and Geometric vases and smaller items, Archaic votive offerings from the temple of Hera in Tiryns (wall cases, left of rear), earthenware ceremonial masks and votive shields from Tiryns (8th century B.C.), Archaic idols and votive offerings, black-figured and red-figured vases (mostly of the 5th century B.C.), Hellenistic pottery, and by the door, an earthenware bathtub with a seat. In the middle row are some panathenaic amphorae and a white lekythos.

## THE POPULAR ARTS AND CRAFTS MUSEUM

The Popular Arts and Crafts Museum of Nauplia is situated at 1, Vassileos Alexandrou Street, on the ground floor of a neo-Classical building. It contains local traditional costumes, jewelry, weapons, tools and utensils from eastern Peloponnesus (including Tsakonia) and from Hydra, old maps of Nauplia, various copper engravings and some photographs of historic monuments which no longer exist.

*78. Mycenaean armour found in the grave of Dendra. It consists of bronze bands, joining the metal plates that covered the chest, neck and shoulders. 15th century B.C.*

79. *Mycenaean bridge-spouted jug, found at Mycenae. It is decorated with the double axe and the sacred knot. 1450-1400 BC.*

80. *Mycenaean jug with painted ornamentation. 1580-1450 B.C.*

81. *Mycenaean jug with painted ornamentation, consisting of floral motifs. 1580-1450 B.C.*

82. *Mycenaean jug found in a grave at Mycenae, with painted ornamentation, consisting of plant motifs and circlets. The design is obviously copied from a metal original. 1580 -1450 B.C.*

83. *Terracotta figurine of a woman from Mycenae. The body is stylized, and there are necklaces and bracelets painted on the neck and arms. 13th century B.C.*

*84. Clay head of a figurine from Asine. The distinctive features — pointed nose and chin (possibly indicating a beard) rounded eyes — give the face a very striking appearance. It is thought to be a nobleman and is known as the "Lord of Asine". 13th century B.C.*

*85. Archaic terracotta figurine of an enthroned figure, found at Tiryns. The figure is stylized and adorned with broad bands that are held together at the shoulders with disc-shaped buckles. There are faint traces of paint.*

*86. Late Archaic terracotta figurine of an enthroned figure, found at Tiryns. The figure is draped in a peplos and adorned with ribbons. The face is modelled in fine detail.*

87. *Fresco of a woman, found at Mycenae. She is wearing typical created head-dress of a princess and holding wheat-stalks in her hands. 13th century B.C.*

88. *Mycenaean painted terracotta figurine, found at Mycenae. 13th century B.C.*

# EPIDAURUS

In a small valley above the port of old Epidaurus, 29 km. east of Nauplia, the ancient sanctuary of Asclepios was founded and subsequently developed into probably the largest healing center of antiquity. About half-way (14.5 km.) on the modern motorway which skirts the southern foot-hills of Arachnaion, at the entrance and exit of the Aghios Ioannis (Arkadiko) community, there is a Mycenaean road *bridge* and a *tholos tomb* of which the dromos and the back portion of the tholos have survived. The course of the ancient road therefore, although more narrowly conforming to the contours of the land, must not have been too different from the modern one.

Asclepios, according to legend, was the son of Apollo and Coronis, a mortal; initially a hero, he was later deified and was included in the Thessalic pantheon. We have no way of knowing how the worship of Asclepios was transplanted to Epidaurus (clearly, the relative mythological variations were invented later); but it is interesting to note that in order for it to take root, it was necessary to identify Asclepios with a local form of Apollo, himself merged already into a still earlier deity, Maleatas (see below). Thus the earliest installations of the sanctuary date as late as the 6th century B.C. while Asclepios continued until much later to be mentioned together with Apollo Maleatas. In the 5th century B.C. the healing center had become known outside the limits of Epidauria, especially after the plague epidemic of Athens and the establishment of the Asclepieion at the foot of the Acropolis in 419 B.C. The center reached its peak at the end of the 4th and the beginning of the 3rd century B.C. (370-250 B.C.) when it became a place of a panhellenic pilgrimage and some of its more important buildings were erected. In the 2nd century A.D. it underwent more renovation, especially thanks to the generosity of the Roman senator Antoninus. It continued operating until 426 A.D., at which time Emperor Theodosius II had it closed, along with all other pagan sanctuaries.

Whatever the origins of the worship of Asclepios may be, he has all the basic characteristics of a chthonian (nether world) deity, combined with nature's annual cycle of decline and regeneration. His symbol was the serpent — the

89. *The best preserved ancient Greek theatre: Epidaurus. Beginning of the 3rd century* B.C.

90. *General view of the sanctuary of Asclepios at Epidaurus, seen from Mt. Tithion, with* ▶ *the theatre in the background.*

animal whom the ancients conceived as living above and, at the same time, within the earth; of all the qualities attributed to the chthonic deities, that which prevailed in the serpent was healing; this belief was based on the deities' familiarity with vegetation in general and with therapeutic herbs in particular, as well as on their power over the undeterminate forces of the nether world which communicate with living organisms in a mysterious, magical way and affect their condition and development. After certain ritual cleansings, the sick would spend the night in a special building, the *enkoimeterion* (sleeping ward), where the god would appear in their dreams and suggest the treatment they should follow. Not excluding surgery and drug treatment completely, therapy at the Asclepieion relied mainly on the patient's shattering psychical experience, the shock of having come into direct contact with the supernatural — an experience which, in psychogenic and nervous disorders especially, must have given immediate and impressive results. Treatment was not provided free of charge, but payment could be quite minimal. The *Asclepieia* festival was instituted at the beginning of the 5th century B.C.; this panhellenic feast was held every four years and included theatrical performances as well as athletic and, later, musical competitions; however, the Asclepieia could never boast of the brilliance that had marked the games at Olympia, Delphi, Isthmia, and Nemea.

The Asclepieion was excavated by P. Kavvadias (1879-1928, and more thoroughly in 1881-1889). J. Papademetriou did additional research on the sanctuary of Maleata (1948-1951), where excavations were resumed in 1974.

The motorway does not take us to the original entrance of the sanctuary which was on the north side, but rather to the south side of the site where there are the auxiliary installations of the sanctuary, at some distance from the sacred precinct. If the modern visitor, therefore, does not wish to cross the entire area first and then explore it by slowly retracing his steps to the point of departure, he must take direction completely opposed to that used in ancient times; the description which follows is adapted to this latter course.

Just off the entrance to the archaeological site and the Museum (see below) and continuing right towards the slopes of Mt. Kynortion, one comes upon the **theatre,** perhaps the most famous of the ancient world. Preserved almost intact, it was restored wherever necessary (especially at the sides), and is in use today. By all indications, it was built at the beginning of the 3rd century B.C., and therefore not by Polycleitus the Younger, as tradition would have it. It originally had 34 rows of seats built of limestone, divided into 12 sections, and a seating capacity of 6000. In the 2nd century B.C. the upper part was extended to accommodate an addition to the auditorium by which 21 rows of seats divided into 22 sectors, built on an artificial earth fill were erected, bringing the total seating capacity to 12,000. The seats of the front row, reserved for dignitaries, differed from the rest in that they were built of a reddish stone and had a support for the back. The *orchestra,* 20.30 m. in diameter, is encircled by a narrow strip of marble, its floor is of packed earth, and it has a *thymele* (altar) in the middle (of which only the circular base has survived). One came to the orchestra and the auditorium by two *parodoi* (the double poros stone door frames are restorations). Behind the orchestra was the *skene* (scene) building of which only the foundations remain. Originally, it was in the shape of a hypostyle stoa with a row of pillars and a parapet at the rear, four internal colonnades and double rooms on either side. The *proscenium,* 22 m. long and 3.17 m. wide, had two low wings which projected forward by 1 m. at either extremity and 14 Ionic half-columns

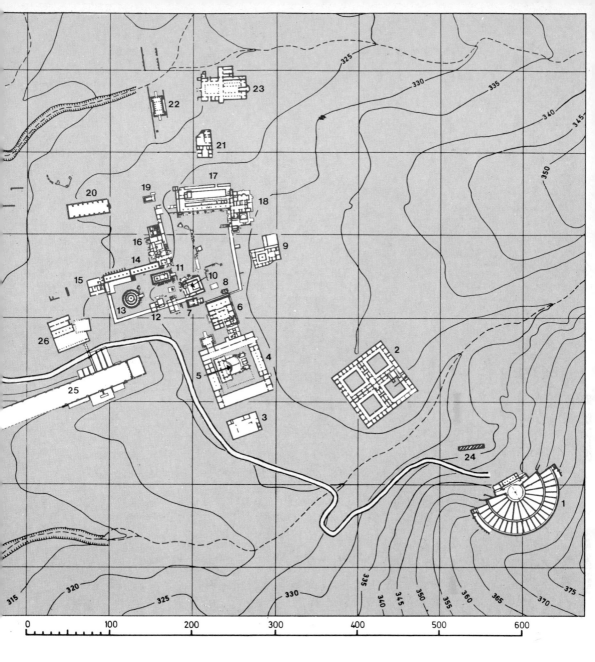

## Plan of Epidaurus

1. Theatre
2. Xenon (Hostel or Katagogion)
3. Bath
4. Gymnasium
5. Odeum
6. Palaistra, stoa of Kotys
7. Temple of Artemis
8. Temple of Themis
9. Temple of Asclepios and Apollo of the Egyptians
10. House for the Priests
11. Temple of Asclepios
12. Buildings
13. Tholos
14. Sleeping ward or abaton
15. Fountain
16. Bath and library
17. Stoa
18. Roman bath
19. Temple of Aphrodite
20. Cistern
21. Mansion
22. Propylaia
23. Christian basilica
24. Museum
25. Stadium
26. Hostel for athletes and palaistra

131

91. The theatre of Epidaurus, the most famous ancient theatre in Greece, which has survived almost intact. The photograph shows the orchestra, the tiers of seats (Kerkides), one of the chorus entrances (parodoi) and the remains of the scene building (Skene).

92. *The sanctuary of Asclepios, showing the Gymnasium — a large square structure with well constructed ashlar exterior walls.*

on façade. At the time when the actors still moved around within the orchestra itself the space between these half-columns was used for installing revolving triangular boards, the *periacta,* which carried painted stage sets. When the theater was extended, the skene too was enlarged by the addition of a quadrilateral area on the west side and the blocking of the openings between the pillars of the rear wall. In the meantime the actors had begun to perform on the skene itself, leaving the orchestra to the chorus, and the sets were shifted to the walls of the skene. In A.D. 267 Alaric's Visigoths destroyed the theater as well as the whole of the sanctuary; later on, all kinds of materials were used to repair the damage. The theater of Epidaurus is famous for its perfect acoustics: the smallest sound — a deep breath or the tearing of a piece of paper — can be heard clearly as high up as the last row of seats.

Coming down from the theater, one goes past the Museum, crosses a dry stream-bed and reaches a level clearing where the sanctuary buildings are erected. The first building one encounters is the **xenon** or hostel (otherwise known as the *katagogion*) a square 76.30 × 76.30 m. structure built in the 4th century B.C. to accommodate the pilgrims. The xenon had two floors and 160

93. *The Roman odeum at Epidaurus, with its semicircular orchestra and the substructure of the seats.*

rooms built around four large square courtyards with Doric colonnades. What remains is the lower course of the walls (polygonal limestone constructions built on poros stone foundations), the thresholds of the rooms, the stylobates of the colonnades and a few segments of columns. Nothing of the brick superstructure has survived. West of the xenon, there are the walls of another, somewhat later, quadrilateral building (early 3rd century B.C.); here one can also see remains of a later brick floor and the bases of an internal colonnade which crossed it lengthwise (E-W). The building was divided into several rooms; the bathtubs and wash basins found here suggest that this was a **bath installation** of the Greek period, perhaps related to the xenon but also to its neighbouring and contemporaneous **gymnasium** — a large structure (76×70 m.) with well constructed ashlar exterior walls built on poros stone foundations. Initially the gymnasium had an inner peristyle court consisting of 60 columns, hypostyle platforms on the east and west sides, stoas on the north and south sides, and rooms at the corner ends. The entrance, on the north-western corner, was built as a propylon (the flag stones survive) with 6 Doric columns on its façade and 4 more on either side. The mud brick superstructure of the building has not been preserved.

94. *Reconstruction of the sanctuary of Asclepios at Epidaurus, showing the temple of*

On the site of the propylon the Romans built a small **temple of Hygeia** (the daughter of Asclepios) and a small **odeum** on the site of the inner court; the odeum had a semi-circular orchestra, mosaic floor, brick proscenium with two shallow niches on the façade, anf two parodoi on either side. The seats have not been preserved but one can still see their substructure of brick and other materi-als from earlier structures.

Due north of the gymnasium, there is another smaller building (34.20 × 29.35 m.), quite similarly designed but not as carefully constructed; it was built during the Roman period and repaired later on by Antoninus. It is an almost square structure with an entrance and a shallow propylon on its west side, a hypostyle area in the middle, rooms on its three sides (with a small door on the south side), and a hypostyle stoa on the fourth (north) side. In front of the stoa, stone tables and benches were found dating from an earlier installation. What is left of the exterior walls is built of carefully hewn stones whereas the interior walls are clumsy stone and mortar constructions. Several stone pillars were found *in situ*. The building is generally thought to have been a **palaistra** (or wrestling school) and the stoa on its north side is believed to have been the **stoa of Kotys** mentioned by Paysanias; but if instead of being an open air area the central enclosure had been covered by an elevated roof, it is possible that this was, or had been converted into, some religious club's hall or place of worship.

In front of the structure, sidewise to its north-western corner, we see the remains of the **temple of Artemis;** built at the end of the 4th century B.C., it had

*Asclepios, the tholos and the temple of Artemis in the sacred grove.*

6 Doric columns on its east façade and a floor-paved with evenly cut square limestone slabs on a poros stone foundation. The temple was reached by a ramp, also paved with flagstones, that connected the temple to a small altar in front of it. In the cella of the temple there was a statue of worship surrounded by 10 Corinthian columns. Architectural fragments and pieces from its sculpted decoration may be seen at the Museum.

The **temple of Themis,** east of the temple of Artemis, is quite different: it is a small quadrilateral building (7.25×4.85 m.), also dating from the 4th century B.C., of which only the lower course of the walls is preserved, forming a frame-like structure divided into two by a thin transversal wall. The building had two entrances, one east and one west, with low ramps and pillars at the corners and along its lengths. At an angle from the north-east side of the temple, there is a complex of Roman buildings: a square area which had a Doric stoa on its western façade and a square courtyard behind it, most probably the **temple of Asclepios and Apollo of the Egyptians,** erected by Antoninus. A private mansion with two atriums surrounded by rooms built of various materials was added on the south side of the temple.

Coming back westwards, the visitor enters the sacred grove, the very center of worship, where women were not allowed to give birth nor men to die; the area was encircled by boundary stones which, however, have disappeared. The first building that one encounters lies at the south-east corner of the site. It is a square structure (24.30×20.70 m.), slightly aslant to the enclosure and the other build-

ings, with long and narrow rooms along its sides. Only its poros stone foundations and parts of the bottom course of the walls have survived. It is the oldest
building of the sanctuary. A small temple and altar of Apollo had initially been
erected in the north-west corner of this site. But by the 6th century B.C. Asclepios had replaced Apollo as the major figure of worship and the small temple
had been incorporated into the building which from 550 B.C. onwards served as
the Asclepieion's sleeping ward. Later on it apparently fell into disuse, and still
later the Romans converted it into a *house for the priests*. From here a stone
paved road led to an **altar** which continued to belong to Apollo even after the
temple had disappeared.

North of the altar stood the **temple of Asclepios** of which very little has been
preserved: the completely ruined poros stone foundations (24.30×13.20 m.), a
portion of the substructure of the pronaos floor, and the ramp at the east façade.
It was built in 490 B.C. by the architect Theodotus in the Doric order, with 6
columns on the fronts and 11 columns on the flanks. The pediment sculptures
(Battle of the Amazons and Battle of the Centaurs or the Fall of Troy) and the
pediment ornaments were done by the sculptor Timotheos the Epidaurian. The
gold and ivory statue of worship, the work of Thrasymedes from Paros, stood at
the rear of the cella in a cavity measuring 2.70×1.75 m. and 0.58 m. deep, i.e.
below floor level — a characteristic feature of statues of oracles and gods of
healing. In front of the temple is the altar and a paved road leading to it. Just off
the temple there are some semi-circular platforms erected by private individuals
as offerings to the god; west of the house of the priests, over the south wall of the
enclosure, there is a Classical building whose function has not been determined.

Behind the temple, at the rear of the enclosure (supported on the west side
by a strong retaining wall, built of segments of columns and other old materials)
is the **tholos,** of which only the basement has survived (21.82 m. diameter). It
consists of three concentric circular walls, built of ashlar blocks. The circles
intercommunicate by narrow openings on varying axes but this does not make a
passage so complicated as to call it a labyrinth. The outer circle is surrounded by
a foundation of reddish soft poros stone which supported the three-tiered platform of the building accesible by a ramp on the east side. The tholos was
circular. It was built of white marble and had an exterior Doric colonnade of 26
columns which rested on the outer circle of the basement and supported a frieze
with sculpted rosettes; the wall of the tholos rested on the second basement
circle and had a door opening to the east (its frame, richly decorated with
sculpted ornaments, may be seen in the Museum). Finally there was an internal
Corinthian colonnade of 14 pillars resting on the inner circle. The colonnades
supported a coffered ceiling with floral decoration. The floor consisted of alternating black and white slabs (see reconstruction at the Museum); in its middle
there was a round opening covered with a mobile white slab which communicated with the basement. The inner surface of the wall was richly decorated by
the painter Pausias. The tholos is believed to have been the work of Polycleitus
the Younger, built in 360-330 B.C. Although certainly a place of worship, its
precise function is not known; in any event it must have been related to the
chthonic character of the god and most probably the basement and its circular
passages were the abode of Asclepios's sacred serpents.

To the north, the enclosure is flanked by the **sleeping ward** or **abaton** where
the sick would lie down hoping that the form of their therapy would be revealed
to them in their dreams; it was a stoa, 70 m. long and 5.50 m. wide, with 29 Ionic
columns on the south façade and 13 internal posts. The spaces between the

95. *Cross-section of the temple of Asclepios, with a reconstruction of the chryselephantine statue of the god.*

columns were filled by low parapets. Because the soil sloped downwards to the west, the earlier east section of the stoa (4th century B.C.) is an one-storey structure, while the later, west section (3rd century B.C.) has two floors with strong octagonal Doric pillars supporting the floor. Today we can see only the well preserved poros stone bases and some fragments of columns. On the east side of the building there used to be a 6th century B.C. well, 17 m. deep, whose water was believed to have curative qualities. Inscriptions describing various types of therapy were placed around the mouth of the well. This well and the older sleeping ward (see above) are contemporaneous with the earliest stages of the building of the sanctuary.

On the west side of the sleeping ward there is a **fountain** of the Roman period, with rubble walls covered with plaster built on poros stone foundations

*96. The temple of Asclepios. Reconstruction of the east wall of the temple of the god.*

97. *Reconstruction of the tholos, showing the Doric peristyle and the ornamental motifs on the metopes.*

(perhaps Classical). On its façade there used to be a colonnade and, in the rear, a row of narrow quadrilateral rooms (cisterns?), with a larger hall at the far end. Next to it there is a conduit coated with hydraulic mortar. The fountain is outside the enclosure of the sacred grove, as are the buildings described below.

The first of these structures, touching the north-eastern edge of the enclosure, is an extensive building complex of the 2nd century A.D. (its south side has not been excavated yet) consisting of **baths** (north) and a **library** (south), both erected over earlier Greek ruins, possibly places of worship. The foundations, which are the only things that have survived, indicate that the library was divided into quadrilateral rooms with a larger square room in the middle. The complex faces east, overlooking a large open space — a square — whose north side is dominated by a large arcaded structure of the 3rd century B.C. consisting of a long and narrow peristyle court with shops all along its sides. The only surviving features are the foundations, the stone drains for rain water and sewage and the stylobates on which the columns rested. In its better days, however, the building must have looked quite impressive, with Doric colonnades on the exterior, Ionic columns inside, mud brick walls and tiled roof.

On the east side of the square, extending to the south is a large **Roman bath building,** with brick walls built on stone foundations and mosaic floors. One to two meters of the wall's height is preserved. The central hall is paved with marble; the monolithic shafts of the four columns that stood in it have survived. According to one view, this structure was originally used as the sanctuary's water reservoir.

On the southern end of the baths there is a quadrilateral structure with a stoa facing south; in front of this stoa there was an open court with a ramp leading to the entrance, and at the rear a semi-circular platform with pedestals for the statues worshipped. Most probably this was the **Epidoteion,** the sanctuary of the gods of plenty, built in the 4th century B.C. and restored and renovated by Antoninus in the 2nd century A.D.

West of the stoa with the shops stood the small **temple of Aphrodite,** built in 320 B.C. Now the visitor can see nothing but the foundations of soft reddish poros stone disintegrated by time; originally however it had two (or four) Ionic columns on its façade and a cella with an inner Corinthian colonnade along the walls. Beyond the temple there is a large quadrangular **cistern** with buttressed walls of yellowish poros stone coated with plaster. North-east of the cistern there are ruins of a post-Roman building (a bath) and opposite this, to the east, a 5th century A.D. **mansion** (the lower course of the walls and the door jambs are preserved) built after the decline of the sanctuary. Continuing north and coming down the slope, the visitor reaches the old entrance where the ancient road from Epidaurus used to end; these are the sanctuary's **propylaia,** built in 340-330 B.C. (or according to another view, in 300 B.C.). The propylaia is a 20 × 13 m. quadrilateral structure of which only the strong stone foundations have survived, and the ramps leading to its narrow sides. These foundations supported a colonnade (Ionic or Doric) on each of the façades and two side walls with a frieze of bucraniums and rosettes in relief. In the space thus formed, 14 Corinthian columns supported the roof. This arrangement did not allow chariots or loaded animals to enter the propylaia, so that a different entrance must have been used for these.

East of the propylaia, outside the sanctuary enclosure, a large **Christian basilica** with five aisles was built at the end of the 4th or the beginning of the 5th century A.D.; today we can see only the foundations of the walls, the floors, and the rear apse. Various materials from the ruined sanctuary were used in its construction. On its west side it had a large peristyle court with towers at the corners and a gradated entrance in the middle. At the back of the court there was a long and narrow narthex which protruded from the main body of the basilica to the south and to the north where the baptistry had been built. The five aisles (the middle one was the widest) are intersected on the east side by another transversal aisle; the altar niche is in the middle of the back wall. The floors of the basilica were decorated with fine mosaics.

Beyond the fenced archaeological site, to the right of the modern asphalt road, lies the **stadium,** built between two hillocks whose slopes had been levelled to accommodate the spectators. A rectilinear sphendone (narrow side) created by an earth fill on the east edge gave the stadium a square shape. The track is flanked by drains and by small pillars on the sides evenly spaced at 32 m. from each other, and by a row of stone slabs at the start and at the finish; it is 196.44

*98. Remains of the tholos, the remarkable circular structure in the sanctuary of Asclepios at Epidaurus.*

m. long, 23 m. wide, and has a 181.30 m. long course. On the sphendone and on both sides of the stadium there were rows of stone seats arranged into sectors (14 rows on the south side, 22 rows on the north side and 5 rows on the sphendone have been preserved). Under the seats of the north side, an underground vaulted passage, built in the Hellenistic period, connected the stadium to two buildings north of it and west of the sacred enclosure — one is a square peristyle structure and the other a building with rooms, possibly a hostel for the athletes, and a palaistra for their training.

Two kilometers south-east of the Asclepieion, on a low hilltop of Mt. Kynortion, is the **sanctuary of Maleatas,** accessible by a footpath starting from the Asclepieion. It was discovered by P. Kavvadias but actually excavated by J.

*99. Remains of the rectangular stadium at Epidaurus. Some of the tiers of stone seats in the sphendone still survive.*

Papademetriou. This area was inhabited from as early as the 3rd millennium B.C. but the first signs of worship (an altar formed by the accumulated ashes of sacrifices) belong to the 7th century B.C. At the start of the 4th century B.C., a small simple temple was built, with two columns on the façade and marble sculptures; towards the end of the same century, a long stoa with 17 or 19 columns on the façade was added to its north (downhill) side supported by a strong retaining wall reinforced with buttresses. The Romans added a cistern, a fountain and a building with a courtyard, most probably the house of the priest. It is interesting to note that despite Asclepios's identification with Maleatas, this old sanctuary continued to function until the end, along with the new larger, and more famous sanctuary of Asclepios.

# THE MUSEUM OF EPIDAURUS

Returning to the present day entrance to the archaeological site, one may visit the Museum, the final stage of one's tour of the area. A bust of P. Kavvadias, the excavator, is placed just outside the building. Two Ionic columns from the sleeping ward and two Corinthian columns from the interior of the tholos stand along the wall of the Museum's façade.

The *first room* contains inscriptions (tribute to Apollo Maleatas and Asclepios, offered at the beginning of the 3rd century B.C. by the Epidaurian poet Isyllos, report on the construction of the temple of Asclepios and of the tholos, description of therapies), a collection of medical instruments, a plaster cast of a votive relief offered by someone suffering of an ear disease (the original of this and of several other sculptures from Epidaurus are in the National Archaeological Museum of Athens) and, high up on the wall, decorative roof tiles from various buildings of the sanctuary.

In the *second room* there are plaster copies of statues of Asclepios, Hygeia, and other sculptures and votive offerings, a reproduction of the frieze of the gymnasium propylon, various architectural pieces and some sculptured ornaments from the top and the edges of the pediment of the temple of Asclepios, and several female figures on horseback (known as the "Aurai" or Breezes).

The *third room* contains the most impressive exhibits of the Museum: sculptures from the temple of Artemis (especially statues of victories), the reconstruction of a corner section from the temple of Asclepios (exterior colonnade, wall and internal colonnade) and fragments from the sculptured decoration of the temple. At the back of the room there are partially restored sections of the floor of the tholos, of the frieze with the rosette decoration, and the marvellous Corinthian capital known for its excellent analogies and fine workmanship and believed to be the work of Polycleitus the Younger. Set against the right wall are fragments of the tholos roof with some exquisite floral sculptures and in the niches one sees the finely decorated frame of the tholos door and a replica of the frieze from the temple of Artemis.

In a special small building near the Museum one can see the inscriptions found on the site and the area of Epidaurus.

*100. Epidaurus Museum: a Corinthian capital renowned for its symmetry and exquisite stonework. It is believed to be the work of Polycleitos the Younger.*

*101. Interior of the Epidaurus Museum: restored sections of the interior of the tholos and* ▶ *of its ornamentation, and sculptured fragments belonging to various structures in the sanctuary.*

*102. Epidaurus Museum: an example of the ornamentation on the tholos door, with skilfully carbed rosettes.*

*103-104. The coffered ceiling panels of the peristyle surrounding the tholos, remarkable for the beautiful, life-like flowers. Their sensitive modelling ranks them among the most exquisite designs ever used in architectural ornamentation.*

103

104

# FINDS FROM EPIDAURUS
# IN THE NATIONAL ARCHAEOLOGICAL MUSEUM
# OF ATHENS

The sculptures from the sanctuary of Asclepios at Epidaurus have been brought together in the National Archaeological Museum in Athens. Most of them are housed in a single room (the Epidaurus Room) and come from the pediments of the temple of Asclepios.

The expressiveness of the figures in these fragmentary pedimental compositions reveals that the artist who carved them was not afraid of radical innovation; and the light figures of Nereids and Aures from the akroteria of the temple formed very elegant crowning members for this imposing building.

The same room houses fragments of the Dorian *peristasis* from the tholos, part of which is restored in the Museum at Epidaurus; there are pieces of the *sima*, with maeander decoration, and gargoyles in the shape of lion's heads with open mouths and hollow eyes. There are also three figures from the temple of Artemis, on stands, and flying Victories (Nikes), executed with considerable skill and with a joyous, fresh spirit.

*105. Akroterion from a pediment of the temple of Asclepios at Epidaurus. A woman with a beautiful body and elaborate draperies — a Nereid or an Aura — is seated upon a horse, probably rising from the sea. 380 B.C.*

106. Small statue of a bearded Asclepios, found in the sanctuary of Asclepios at Epidaurus. The god is wearing short himation and leaning on a staff with a serpent entwined round it. The statue has been carved with great care: the limbs are beautifully balanced and the face has an intensely spiritual expression. Early 4th century B.C.

107. Headless statue of amazon on horseback. She is wearing a short chiton and hunting boots. In one hand she is brandishing a spear above a fallen warrior, who lies under the hooves of her rearing horse. It was found at Epidaurus.

*108. Ruins of the acropolis of ancient Asine.*

# MIDEA - ASINE - LERNA

## MIDEA

The motorway east of Argos goes through Merbaka (now named Aghia Trias, where there is a 12th century Byzantine church with built-in fragments from the Heraion and where, during the Turkish occupation, the Archbishop of Nauplia used to have his seat), on to Dendra village, and thence to Manesi. At a road turning, where some plane-trees surround a spring and the chapel of Aghios Thomas, there is a foot-path that takes you up to the top of a steep conical hill where the ancient **Mycenaean acropolis** of Midea used to be. The Cyclopean walls, probably built at the beginning of the 14th century B.C., surround the northern, western and south-western side of the hill; they are 5.50–7 m. thick, and (in places they have been repaired in Hellenistic times) have been preserved to 7 m. of their total height. The eastern and south-eastern slopes are so steep that no walls had to be built. There are two *entrances* to the fortifications: a western one, between a bastion (formed by a turn of the wall) and the steep side of the rock; and an eastern gate, 2 m. wide, with a stepped threshold, situated opposite the western entrance. At the hilltop, the Swedish Archaeological Institute discovered remains of foundations believed to be those of a palace. At other points, retaining walls and various buildings were located, but not excavated except for some trial shafts which revealed destruction by fire at the end of the 12th century B.C.

About 1 km. west of the acropolis and 200 m. beyond the village Dendra, one *tholos tomb* and twelve *chamber tombs* were found which contained many intact burials. The finds (weapons, jewelry, vases and utensils, many of them in gold and silver) are some of the most brilliant examples of Mycenaean civilization; except for a complete bronze armour of a Mycenaean warrior now at the Nauplia Museum, all the rest is exhibited at the National Archaeological Museum of Athens.

## ASINE

Nine kilometers south-east of Nauplia is the bay of Tolon; its eastern arm is dominated by a rocky hill, the Kastraki or ancient Asine, which was excavated by the Swedish Archaeological Institute. The area was inhabited since Middle Helladic and Mycenaean times; main finds include tombs (on the eastern slope of neighbouring Barbouna hill) and remains of houses which, however, have been covered up again. But the fortifications of the hill have been preserved and are clearly visible. They consist of an almost uninterrupted wall of the Hellenistic period into which a *Geometric tower,* built of large uncut blocks of stone, has been incorporated in its south-eastern side. The entrance is on the north-eastern slope and is flanked by two polygonal *towers*; the east tower has a 10 m. wide

*109. Ancient Lerna. Part of the excavated area.*

façade and 9.50 m. of its height has been preserved, while the west tower was repaired and partially rebuilt by the Venetians. *The gate* between these two towers has a 2 m. long and 0.50 m. wide threshold. The gate is reached by a gradated ramp whose bottom portion was destroyed when a *Roman bath* was built across it (part of its underground heating installation has been preserved). Within the entrance there is a semi-circular levelling carved into the rock, a kind of courtyard; behind it, along the wall, one can see the foundations of a Roman building with a square antechamber which leads to a large hypostyle room. Above this entrance and the building stands a ruined *Venetian tower*.

The fortifications of this hill were built to protect a Hellenistic township, nothing of which remains today.

## LERNA

Ancient Lerna (now Myloi, so called because of the many watermills operating during the Turkish occupation and after) lies 12 km. from Argos, on the road to Tripoli. The section between the seashore and the foot-hills of mount Pontinos is narrow and soggy from the once neighbouring lake Alkyonis and the marshes. Here, according to legend, lived the Lernean Hydra, the nine-headed monster slain by Heracles (some people believe that the poisonous monster symbolized the malarial diseases that used to harass the area). Here too in 1825, General Makriyannis checked Ibrahim's advance, thus allowing the Naupliots to prepare the defense of the city. Today Lerna is still abundantly supplied with water but the marshes have been reclaimed and the area is full of plane-trees and citrus fruit orchards. In one of these orchards, half orange grove and half farmland, the ancient settlement of Lerna was discovered; it was founded in Neolithic times, flourished in the Early Bronze Age (Early Helladic) and was inhabited up to the Geometric period. It was excavated by an American archaeological mission, under J. Caskey. Most of the excavated area has been refilled and covered up, but the main and most representative structures were retained above ground, and some of them are kept under a specially constructed shelter.

At the southern end of the site, one can see the double wall of the Early Helladic settlement with two neighbouring semi-circular **towers** and some stone steps at the bottom of the western tower. The lower course of the wall is constructed of large uncut stones, its upper course was made of mud bricks. Originally, a stout retaining wall served as a fortification (a small uneven fragment of it is visible between the two façades of the wall next to the western tower). The outer line of fortifications was built later on, along with the towers and the steps which led to a gate higher up in the wall. Finally, the inner line of fortifications and the transversal walls which connect it to the outer line were added, and the tower was remodelled into a quadrangular structure. West of the towers and the gate, the wall rested on an older **Neolithic** quadrangular **house** with walls of rubble masonry strengthened by buttresses. East and north-east of the towers there are sections of **Middle Helladic houses** (1900-1600 B.C.); one of them had square rooms containing cooking utensils, the other was horseshoe shaped and had been built in two successive stages; its walls had been faced with clay and it was presumably a bronze foundry.

The ruler's mansion (a roofed 12×25 m. structure) is certainly the most impressive of the lot. It is known as the **House of Tiles** because of the amount of schist and clay roof-tiles found among the debris. Its entrance, a long and narrow hallway, is on the north-eastern side. Then come two square rooms which alternate with two other long and narrow rooms; interior corridors run along the length of the mansion. By the door of the third room, facing the southern corridor, there are some steps which suggest that there was a second floor and that the corridor was in fact a staircase. The lower courses of the walls are stone, the higher ones mud bricks. The walls are faced with clay or with 2-3 layers of some kind of stucco decorated with large square borders (the closely-set wavy carvings on the clay facing on the interior of the rooms were not intended as decorations, but rather as a preparation for the stucco, which however was never applied). Towards the end of the Early Helladic period (2300-2200 B.C.) the mansion was completely destroyed by fire. The debris were gathered and piled carefully in a mound which covered its walls. Many centuries later, about 1600 B.C., large shaft graves (similar to the royal tombs of Mycenae) were dug at Lerna; one of these was dug next to the mound, another one inside it. Apart from the graves, the area is full of pits opened in later periods, mostly rubbish dumps which lend an untidy aspect to the site.

# BIBLIOGRAPHY

BLEGEN, C., *The Mycenaean Age,* Cincinatti, 1962.
— *Prosymna, The Argive settlement preceding the Argive Heraeum,* Cambridge, 1937.
CASKEY, J., Preliminary reports on excavations at Lerna, *Hesperia* 1954-1959.
COURBIN, P., *La céramique géométrique de l'Argolide,* Paris, 1966.
— *Les tombes géométriques d'Argos,* Paris, 1974.
DESBOROUGH, V.R. D'A., *The last Mycenaeans and their successors,* Oxford, 1964.
FRÖDIN, O—A. PERSSON, *Asine,* Stockholm, 1938.
GERKAN, A. VON.—W. MÜLLER - WIENER, *Das Theater von Epidauros,* Stuttgart, 1961.
GRUBEN, G., *Die Tempel der Griechen,* München, 1966.
KARO, G. *Führer durch die Ruinen von Tiryns,* Athen, 1934.
KAVVADIAS, P., *Fouilles d'Épidaure,* Athènes, 1891.
LESCHAT, H.—A. DEFRASSE, *Épidaure. Restaurations et description des principaux monuments du sanctuaire d'Asclépios,* Paris, 1895.
MARINATOS, S.—H. HIRMER, *Kreta und das Mykenische Hellas,* München, 1959.
MYLONAS, G., *Mycenae and the Mycenaean Age,* Princeton, 1966.
— *Mycenae: a guide to its ruins and its history,* Athens 1973
— Ὁ ταφικὸς κύκλος Β τῶν Μυκηνῶν, Ἀθῆναι, 1972
PERSSON, A.W., *Royal tombs at Dendra,* Lund, 1931.
— *New tombs at Dendra,* Lund, 1932.
RODENWALDT, G.— K. MÜLLER, *Tiryns, Ausgrabungen des Deutschen Archäologischen Institut in Athen, 1912-1938.*
ROUX, G., *L'Architecture de l'Argolide aux IV et III siècles,* Paris, 1961.
TAYLOUR, W.L, *The Mycenaeans,* London, 1964.
TSOUNTAS, CHR., Μυκῆναι καὶ Μυκηναϊκὸς πολιτισμός, Ἀθῆναι, 1897.
VERMEULE, E., *Greece in the Bronge Age,* Chicago, 1964.
WACE, A.J.B., *Mycenae, an Archaeological History and Guide,* Princeton, 1949.
WACE, H., *Nauplia,* Athens 1964
— *Mycenae Guide,* Athens, 1971.

*The publishers of this guide wish to express their warmest thanks to Professor George Mylonas, of the Academy of Athens, for allowing them to use and publish for the first time his plan of the acropolis of Mycenae. They also wish to thank the French School at Athens for permission to publish ground plans of the archaelogical site at Argos. Thanks are also due to the Athens Centre of Ekistics for permission to use and publish the topographical plans of the acropolis of Mycenae and the sanctuary of Epidaurus.*

*The photographs of M. Chuzeville Nos. 2, 3 are published by permission of the Musée du Louvre, Paris and the photographs Nos. 1, 4 by permission of the Kunsthistorisches Museum, Vienna.*

*The coloured reconstructions of buildings and monuments at Mycenae, the Argive Heraion, Tiryns and Epidaurus are by the painter Stam. Vassiliou.*